D1565375

A Frontier Documentary

A Frontier Documentary

Sonora and Tucson
1821–1848

Edited by
Kieran McCarty

With a Foreword by
James E. Officer

The University of Arizona Press
Tucson

Publication of this book is made possible in part by the proceeds of a permanent endowment created with the assistance of a Challenge Grant from the
National Endowment for the Humanities, a federal agency.

The University of Arizona Press
Copyright © 1997
The Arizona Board of Regents

⊚ This book is printed on acid-free, archival-quality paper.
Manufactured in the United States of America
02 01 00 99 98 97   6 5 4 3 2 1

Library of Congress Cataloging-in-Publication Data

A frontier documentary : Sonora and Tucson, 1821–1848 / edited by
    Kieran McCarty.
        p.   cm.
    Includes bibliographical references and index.
    ISBN 0-8165-1715-0 (cloth : alk. paper)
        1. Tucson (Ariz.)—History—Sources.   2. Sonora (Mexico : State)—
    History—Sources.   3. Southwest, New—History—To 1848—Sources.
    4. Indians of North America—Wars—Arizona—Tucson Region—Sources.
    5. Indians of North America—Missions—Arizona—Tucson Region—
    History—Sources.   I. McCarty, Kieran.
    F819.T957F76   1997
    979.1'776—dc21   97-4576
                                                                  CIP

British Library Cataloguing-in-Publication Data
A catalogue record for this book is available from the British Library.

 Contents

To Thomas Gelsinon,
editor and friend

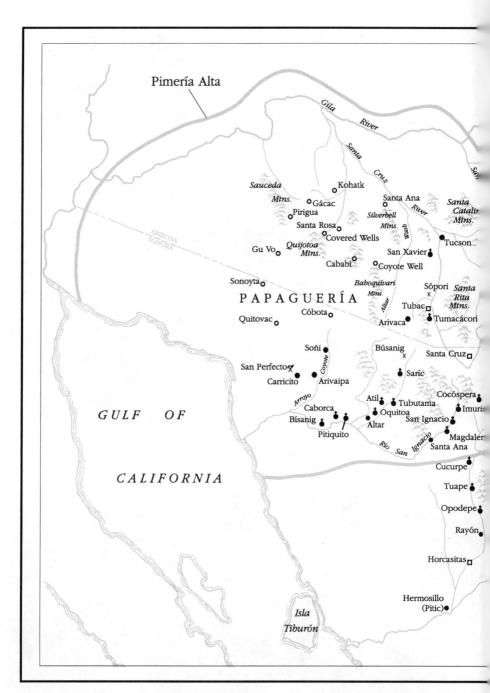

The Mexican state of Occidente, which in 1830 was divided to become Sinaloa and Sonora. (Map by Susan A. Martin)

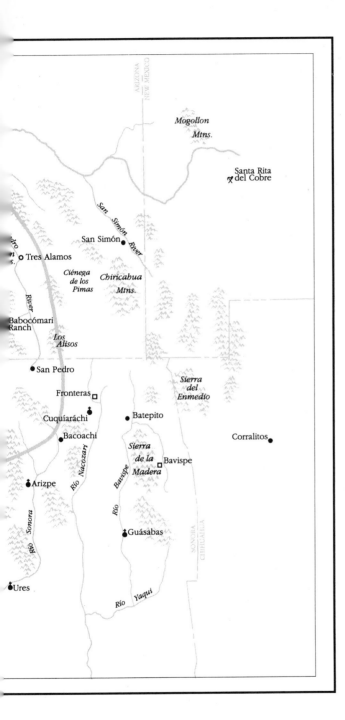

Mogollon Mtns.

Santa Rita del Cobre

San Simón River

San Simón

Tres Alamos

Ciénega de los Pimas

Chiricahua Mtns.

River

Babocómari Ranch

Los Alisos

San Pedro

Fronteras

Sierra del Enmedio

Cuquíaráchi

Batepito

Bacoachi

Corralitos

Río Nacozari

Sierra de la Madera

Río Bavispe

Bavispe

Arizpe

Río Sonora

Río

Guásabas

Ures

Río Yaqui

SONORA / CHIHUAHUA

Key

o   Indian Village

●   Town

□   Presidio

♦   Mission Town

x   Ranch

⚒   Mining Camp

0   miles   50

Foreword

For people interested in the late Spanish colonial history of Arizona, 1976 was a banner year. The University of Arizona Press published two major works and the Arizona Historical Society a third. From the Press came *Friars, Soldiers and Reformers*, John L. Kessler's excellent account of the Tumacácori mission during its administration by the Franciscans, and *Spanish Colonial Tucson*, Henry F. Dobyns's equally brilliant description of the final half century of Spanish rule in southern Arizona. Complementing both was *Desert Documentary: The Spanish Years, 1767–1821*, by Kieran McCarty, O.F.M., and published as the Arizona Historical Society's Historical Monograph Number 4.

McCarty's manuscript differed somewhat from those of Kessel and Dobyns in that he constructed it entirely around a number of original Spanish-language documents he had translated into English. One finds abundant translation of all or parts of original documents in both of the other works, but neither Dobyns nor Kessel focused so completely on describing historical events in the words of those who took part in and wrote about them as did McCarty.

People with little or no knowledge of Spanish colonial history found themselves fascinated with documents such as those in which Juan Bautista de Anza described his early military career, Father Francisco Garcés wrote of a major Apache attack on the mission community of San Xavier in 1769, and Colonel Hugo O'Conór set forth the details of his decision to locate a Spanish military post at the site of modern Tucson in 1775. They also learned the details of Tucson's first murder trial from the letters of Lieutenant Manuel de León.

In concluding his book, McCarty translated from original service records information about the careers of ordinary soldiers serving in the Tubac and Tucson military garrisons. Importantly, these records revealed the role played by early Arizonans in helping the Spanish Crown resist the insurgents who were seeking independence from Mexico between 1810 and 1818.

Shortly after the publication of *Desert Documentary*, Father McCarty advised his friends that he was planning a second volume that would focus on critical documents from the Mexican period of southern Arizona's history. In 1980, after finishing a manuscript on the arrival of Franciscan missionaries in this region, he set to work.[1] Completion of the second manuscript to the author's satisfaction has taken longer than both he and his friends had hoped it would, but all of us are pleased to know that the other shoe is now about to drop.

In the present volume, readers learn from translated Spanish documents about the reconstruction of Tucson's *presidio* wall in the late 1820s; the success of civilian militias in fighting Apaches during the 1830s; conflicts between To-hono O'odham villagers and Mexicans in the 1840s; and the fascinating if tragic life of José Cosme de Urrea, who was baptized and reared in Tucson before going on to become one of the major figures of early nineteenth century Mexican politics. I invite you to read, enjoy, and learn about the history of Arizona and Sonora between 1821 and 1848 from the excellent translations Father McCarty has provided.

James E. Officer

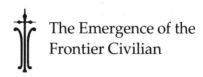

The Emergence of the Frontier Civilian

An Introduction

The Mexican period of Arizona history started much like the "new beginning" in my volume on the years 1767 to 1821, when the spectacular Anza expeditions to California eclipsed routine events on the local Sonoran scene. Shortly after ushering the Tucson *presidio* into the era of Mexican independence in 1821, Captain José Romero strove to reopen Anza's historic overland route to California and to begin regular mail service between Arizpe and Monterey. Like Juan Bautista de Anza before him, Romero was promoted to lieutenant colonel upon reaching California. His exploits, like Anza's, enjoyed wide publicity in Sonora and California, and as far away as Mexico City. They succeeded in distracting later historians from a development of much greater moment: the establishment of representative government within what is now Arizona and the emergence of the frontier civilian.

Because of frequent Apache incursions from both the north and east, far northern Sonora—including for centuries what is now southern Arizona—was referred to politically as *tierra de guerra*, roughly equivalent to what today we would call a war zone. It was completely dominated by the military. Civilian settlers occupied lands and homes only by virtue of subordination in all things to the military activity of the presidio. The presidial captain was the only authority known to the population, military and civilian alike. In legal cases involving civilians, no matter the sophistication of prosecutors and defense attorneys, the presidial commander was always the judge. In a document on Tucson's first murder trial, in 1814, presented in our first volume (pp. 93–110), details of this arrangement are spelled out.

In northwestern Mexico, the development of any form of civilian government was slow. Its roots began, of course, in events relating to the independence movement in central Mexico. In one of history's frequent paradoxes, the army that was to set Mexico free was assigned, in the autumn of 1820, to Agustín de Iturbide by the viceroy, Juan Ruiz de Apodaca, for the sole purpose of putting down the last of the anti-Spanish insurgents, Vicente Guerrero.

Quite unexpectedly, Iturbide joined his royalist forces with Guerrero's insurgents at Iguala on the road to Acapulco. This alliance led to the Plan de Iguala of February 24, 1821, often referred to as Mexico's Declaration of Independence. Then both armies took the road to Veracruz to meet, at Córdoba, a sympathetic Spanish liberal of Irish descent, General Juan O'Donojú, Mexico's new viceroy. On August 24, 1821, the Treaty of Córdoba was signed by O'Donojú and Iturbide, making Mexico's independence official.

The Treaty of Córdoba set off a chain of events in Mexico City that hindered rather than hastening any form of representative government on the far northern frontier. Provincial delegations appointed from Mexico City were quite ineffective because Mexico City itself was torn apart by factions. Liberals favored a republic, and conservatives wanted a monarchy headed by a European prince. The so-called Iturbide Empire predictably lasted only ten months and ended like a Greek tragedy.

Provincial delegations notwithstanding, the only effective political control over the frontier in our region was exerted by Antonio Narbona, a popular commander of the Tucson presidio earlier in the century and later (in 1820) adjutant inspector at Arizpe for the commandancy general. On September 6, 1821, at Arizpe, he swore loyalty to Mexican Independence at the head of his troops, and with the retreat of his superior, Antonio Cordero, and the royalists to Durango, Narbona inherited the position of political chief and military commander of Sonora.

It was not until November 7, 1823, and the fall of Iturbide that the Constitutional Congress—until then manipulated toward centralism by the emperor, with himself in the center—was able to achieve a federalist majority from among the liberals. Fifteen days later, on November 22, the instrument appeared that would bind Mexico's scattered provinces, which were already talking about definitive but dangerous separation into a mutually supporting federation.

The document, known as the Acta Constitutiva de la Federación, was promulgated on January 31, 1824. It divided Mexico's first federal republic into nineteen states, each with its own government. Sonora and Sinaloa were designated as the single state of Occidente, the State of the West. Their constituent congress at El Fuerte (Sinaloa) was seated on September 12, 1824—quite an accomplishment, since it preceded by twenty-two days the proclamation of the national constitution itself. As its president, the constituent congress of Occidente elected Manuel Escalante of Arizpe, who would loom large in desert history for more than a decade.

Occidente would have to wait well over a year, until November 2, 1825, for its state constitution to be proclaimed and a corresponding state government to be established. Consequently, for the sake of law and order throughout the state, the constituent congress arranged for the establishment of local governments as early as December 1824. Towns of less than three thousand inhabitants (presidial towns such as Tucson, for example) would be governed by a mayor or magistrate of law and order and a town attorney, who doubled as town treasurer. December 19 was set for town elections. Local civilian government, conducted by popularly elected officials, operated for the first time in the long history of presidial towns on the Apache frontier.

We therefore begin the main text of this book with a document that gives us an insight into the daily life of the "Old Pueblo" through a week-by-week report for the month of January 1825 by the first popularly elected civilian mayor of Tucson.

Kieran McCarty

A Frontier Documentary

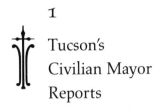

1

Tucson's Civilian Mayor Reports

December 19, 1824, was an unforgettable day in the Old Pueblo. The civilian settlers had been directed by the constituent congress of Occidente to elect by popular vote a civilian mayor of law and order for the settlement, legally independent of the presidial commander. The procedure was unprecedented, but some kind of makeshift voting arrangement was worked out, and José León was legally elected as the first civilian mayor of Tucson.

León took office on January 1, 1825. On February 1 he drew up a report concerning local events that had transpired during his first month in office. His reference to Tucson as a republic gives us an idea of how little the new arrangement was understood, even by the mayor. At the same time, no other document found to date gives us so intimate an insight into the social and cultural life of the Old Pueblo a century and a half ago.

This manuscript is hard to beat as a source of human interest. Events and situations that were taken for granted at the time are totally new and surprising to us. The padre at San Xavier Mission and his running battle with the pueblo's soldiers and settlers over cattle, hotly disputed athletic events between settlers, and raids on the peaceful Apaches made their lives much less drab and boring than we might suspect.

The Republic of Tucson
February 1, 1825

First Week of January

During this week shots were heard out by the horse herd one night. Seventy men went to the rescue: soldiers, settlers, and Pimas from El Pueblito.[1] Although we feared it was an Apache attack, nothing happened. Otherwise, we surely would have lost the horse herd and suffered other casualties due to the disorder of our defenses. Some went out afoot, some riding bareback, and some even unarmed. Signs of the enemy were observed.

Second Week of January

Apaches were sighted in the immediate area. Chief Antuna,[2] assisted by 27 fellow warriors of his company of peaceful Apaches attached to this post, cut off their trail and recovered 17 animals that these same enemy Apaches had stolen from Sonoita in the jurisdiction of Tubac.

Third Week of January

During an off-duty contest of footracing staged between our peaceful Apaches and the local settlers, a suspicion arose that the races had been "fixed." The settlers were angry with the Apaches and demanded the return of their bets. Every effort was made to calm the arguments and hard feelings so that peace might be restored on both sides.

Fourth Week of January

Two soldiers and two settlers had a squabble with the father missionary at San Xavier del Bac. With proper permission and accompanied by a mission cowboy, they had gone hunting on mission lands. They came upon a cow and her unbranded calf. One of the soldiers claimed that they belonged to him.

The cowboy reported to the missionary that the hunters were trying to steal the mission cattle. The missionary called them a pack of thieves, denied all their arguments, and even gave one of them a glancing kick in the shins with the toe of his sandal.

The padre claimed that even if the cattle were stolen, the rightful owner would have to prove it. The padre refused to give up either cow or calf and proceeded to butcher them both at the mission.

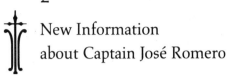

2

New Information
about Captain José Romero

There is no need to repeat here the travel documents of the Romero expeditions to California between 1823 and 1826. In 1962 they were presented in translation and with excellent notes by Lowell J. Bean and William M. Mason in Diaries and Accounts of the Romero Expeditions in Arizona and California, 1823–1826.[1] *But a document in the Provincias Internas section of Mexico's National Archives (the last document in volume 233) provides Romero's earliest military service record and adds half again to our knowledge about Romero and about earlier events preparing him for crossing the Colorado. This document was also published in table form by James E. Officer in* Hispanic Arizona, 1536–1856.[2]

Events immediately leading up to the expedition that left Tucson on June 8, 1823, began earlier when Agustín Fernández, one of Iturbide's delegates to the provincial council of the Californias, authorized one of the Dominican missionaries in Lower California, Fray Félix Caballero, to proceed with Indian guides to Sonora. He left Mission Santa Catalina, near the present international border, on April 4, 1823, and two months later was standing in Arizpe before Antonio Narbona as the first political chief of the Sonoran frontier under Independence.

The important conclusions we draw from Romero's earliest military record are indirect but persuasive. First, that it was Narbona who chose Tucson as the starting point for the expedition and Captain José Romero as its leader. The Tucson escort of a corporal and nine soldiers could also have been handpicked by Narbona, who knew that garrison well as Tucson's most popular commander earlier in the century and who knew Romero as his ensign in the Tucson company from the beginning of the century.

*Then in 1809 Romero was promoted to lieutenant and acting com-
mander of Altar, which kept him in constant touch with Narbona at Tucson and also with the Yumas on the Colorado River to the west. Narbona
chose Romero to lead the expedition because of his spectacular ability to
make friends with the Yuma chiefs along the Colorado between 1809 and
1812, an ability mentioned in his service record. He describes this activity
in the following document and provides us with information that would
be important for the expedition. Romero's success on the frontier explains
his popularity with Narbona, with whom he certainly discussed plans for
the memorable trek to California.*

Opata Company at Bacoachi
December 31, 1817

My name is José Romero, and I am presently a lieutenant commanding the
Opata Indian company at Bacoachi in the Spanish province of Sonora.

I was born in the Oposura Valley in this same province. My age is forty-
one years. My lineage is Spanish. I began my service as a cadet at the royal
presidio of Horcasitas, near where I was born.

The total length of my military service to date is twenty-seven years and
ten months.

On June 6, 1800, I was commissioned as ensign at the presidio of San Agustín del Tucson.

On July 5, 1809, I became the commander of the royal presidio of Santa
Gertrudis de Altar and was promoted to lieutenant, my present grade.

Three years later, on July 1, 1812, I received my present appointment as
commander of the Opata Indian company at Bacoachi, where I have served for
five years and six months.

As commander of the Opatas, I spent a year and eleven months repelling
insurgents from the southern fringe of this province of Sonora.

My total battle record in the military is 18 campaigns and 12 skirmishes.
Sixty-nine of the enemy lost their lives, and in one of the skirmishes I was
seriously wounded.

During my three years at Altar, I was able to make peace with the numerous Yuma nation of the Colorado River, which divides this province of Sonora
from that of California, and secured the friendship of their leaders.

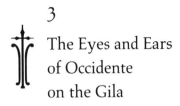

3

The Eyes and Ears
of Occidente
on the Gila

On October 8, 1826, a delegation of Gila Pimas passed through the gates of the Tucson presidio. They were always welcome, for they invariably bore news of importance. In fact, in modern military terms they were an early warning system that was essential for the safety of the Hispanic settlement of Tucson.

Less than a month later, on November 4, Tucson's second constitutional mayor, Ignacio Pacheco, informed the state government by means of the following document of the Pima visit and its aftermath. On this date Pacheco penned the earliest extant record of Mexican awareness of Anglo Americans in Arizona.

Early in the fall of 1826, Old Bill Williams himself was leading a party of beaver trappers down the Gila toward the Colorado. On the way he accepted the hospitality of the Pimas and, of course, regaled them with the usual gifts — mostly such products of eastern manufacturing as knives and axes. It was his visit that the Piman delegation reported. The aftermath is supplied by Pacheco's letter.

What is only suggested in the document, however, is the American interest not only in beaver pelts but in mules and horses as well. The value of Old Bill's gifts far surpassed an overnight stay in a Pima village.

As we see in the document, the Americans asked about mules even before they asked about beaver. The mule, as by far the best mode of transporting pelts, was the backbone of the fur trade. Suspicion ran high that even the loyal Gila Pimas were not above playing middleman between, for example, Old Bill Williams and the Papagos (now the Tohono O'odham), who surreptitiously relieved Mexican ranchos of their mules, which were guarded in turn by the Pimas until an American party came along.

Old Bill Williams's speech to the Gila Pimas, complete with gestures of the ocean waves rolling up onto the continent, reflected the lingering fear at the time of the continuing danger of European powers, including Spain, once again invading western North America and the Gila and Colorado Rivers, none of which yet belonged to the fledgling United States. James Monroe's speech to Congress on December 2, 1823, establishing the Monroe Doctrine bore this out. We are impressed not only that a distant wanderer like Old Bill knew of the Monroe Doctrine—less than three years old—but that he was using it to forge a link between Native Americans and himself.

November 4, 1826

Report to Governor Gaxiola from Tucson

On October 28 the Gila Pimas, represented by a village governor and two of his men, arrived at this presidio with news of 16 foreigners bearing arms along the banks of their river [the Gila]. The Gila governor demanded papers of identification, in lieu of which one or two of their number would have to proceed to this presidio of Tucson to report the destination of their party.

Their leader replied that they came only to visit Indians along the Gila in order to obtain mules and horses from them and to find out where there might be other rivers abounding in beaver.

Manuel de León, our commander, decided to send myself as mayor and Lt. Antonio Comadurán with a detachment of seven men to accompany the village governor and his two companions back to the Gila to meet the strangers and if they were Americans to confront them with the verbal and written orders of our commander general [Simón Elías González] at Arizpe to present themselves there personally before proceeding farther.

We left for this mission on October 30. As the sun was setting on October 31, I came upon seven Indians hunting near the Gila. It was they who informed me that the strangers had left three days earlier, back toward the east.

With Comadurán, I then continued on to the Gila and convoked a meeting of the Pima leaders. They all agreed that the strangers had come with their mules laden with trapping gear for the sole purpose of capturing beaver for their pelts.

They had shown no signs of malice during their four-day stay. On the contrary, they were most friendly and gave many presents of blankets, knives, trays, glass beads, and animals they had trapped.

Their message to our authorities was that they were coming to these villages because Governor Narbona of New Mexico had told them that there were many beaver along these rivers. They had come this first time only to find out for themselves and then return with the proper papers to stay a while. They would bring more presents, for it saddened them to see people so poor, especially since the Indians were such good people.

The strangers then made signs to describe the ocean rolling up on the beach, explaining that people on the other side of that ocean were enemies, enemies of both the white man and the Indian, which made the Indian and the white man brothers.

When the leader of the strangers found out that some Indians had gone to report their presence to the Tucson presidio, he was happy, hoping that they would also report the thievery the Maricopas had inflicted on the strangers, stealing their mules and blankets in broad daylight. A Maricopa dared to steal the captain's own serape.

One of the strangers pointed a gun at the thief, but the captain ordered him to put the gun down. The Maricopas were obviously trying to provoke a fight. Refusing to fall into the trap, the captain told them he did not need the serape and had many more to bring them to gain their friendship. When they finally stole his suitcase—containing his clothing, his papers, and letters from the governor of New Mexico [Narbona]—he gave up trying to win them over and left the village to avoid further confrontation.

The Maricopa who had stolen the suitcase later turned over to me two passports in a foreign language and a letter and a passport signed by the governor of New Mexico. I herewith enclose copies of these documents and am sending the originals to the military commander general in Arizpe.

Lastly, I instructed the Gila Pimas that the moment the strangers returned the Tucson presidio should be advised so as to send word on to the military commander general in Arizpe. Since the strangers seem to be good people, I forbade the Pimas to do them harm and encouraged them to keep the Maricopas from harming these strangers.

Ignacio Pacheco

4

The First
Americans in Tucson

1826

On the last day of the eventful year 1826, three Americans rode into Tucson. Although their names have not been identified, they were the first recorded Americans to visit the Old Pueblo. We might presume that they were the first American trappers dutifully informed by the Gila Pimas either to present proper papers or detour to Tucson personally to report their destination. We know that Old Bill Williams had such papers from Antonio Narbona, governor of New Mexico, and thus avoided the trip to Tucson. These same orders had actually originated much earlier in a circular sent to all frontier posts by Simón Elías González, military commander general at Arizpe.

The American visit was recorded on January 4, 1827, by Juan Romero, Tucson's third constitutional mayor. Romero had replaced Ignacio Pacheco three days before and was sending in a routine report concerning events during December 1826. Besides recording the American visit, Romero confirmed that American fur traders were indeed receiving stolen mules and horses. He also solved the mystery of the Maricopa hostility encountered by Old Bill Williams: Foreigners were looked upon as potential spies traveling downriver to betray Maricopa secrets to their mortal enemies, the Yumas.

Tucson
January 4, 1827

Report to Francisco Iriarte, Governor of Occidente

On the 26th day of December, two Indians from the Gila River came in to report that two parties of Americans had visited their river to trap beaver. The Indians were Gila Pimas and escorted the Americans back up the river because the Maricopas wanted to kill them. The Maricopas also wanted to attack the Papagos who were protecting the Americans.

The Gila Pimas have requested that, for the safety of the Americans, licenses to trap along the Gila not be issued to them. The Maricopas, due to their eternal war with the Yumas, will surely try to kill all Americans. The Papagos accompanied the Americans to protect them from the Maricopas. After the Papagos had returned to their own country, the Maricopas followed the Americans and verified that the Papagos had turned over stolen animals to them.

On the last day of December, three Americans appeared at this presidio to present their passports. They did this in obedience to a letter signed by our commander, Manuel de León, which the Papagos had presented to the Americans. The Americans proceeded no farther than this post.

Juan Romero [rubric]

5

The Old Pueblo in Peril

1827

The late winter and early spring of 1827 were a nightmare for the civilian settlers of Tucson. In its now nearly 220 years of relatively secure existence, the Old Pueblo came closest to complete abandonment in the early part of 1827. Juan Romero, who was just beginning his term as mayor at that time, puts it rather simply in our present document: "We now have no troops here."

Since June 8, 1823, when Tucson's full legal commander, Captain José Romero, with ten of Tucson's regulars, left for more than three years on the California expedition, the local presidio's roster had been riddled with vacancies. In October 1825, General José Figueroa, the new governor of Occidente, added a number of Tucson presidials to his already enormous escort while on his way through the Old Pueblo to rendezvous with Captain Romero and his contingent of Tucsonans at the Colorado River.

The rendezvous never took place. It was not until November 1825 that Governor Figueroa, waiting at the Colorado River for Captain Romero—who would not arrive for another month—got word of the rebellion launched months before in the delta of the Yaqui River by the great Yaqui leader Juan Ignacio Jusacamea, popularly known as Juan de la Bandera. The Yaqui offensive was moving fast into northern Sonora.

By November 29, Figueroa was back in Tucson recruiting most of the garrison for his march south against Juan de la Bandera. At Agua Caliente, southwest of the great bend in the Gila, he left more Tucsonans from his own forces to wait for Romero, who finally crossed the Colorado on December 19.

The Yaqui rebellion was at its height when Tucson's third mayor, Juan Romero, wrote his call for help from the state government. Rumor was *rife that the Yaquis, in the nearly two years of their devastating offensive, had had more than enough time to coordinate an alliance between themselves and the Apaches, the Papagos, and even the Yumas.*

Another factor imperiling Tucson was the formerly protective presidial wall. Not only were all the presidio's troops in the south with Figueroa trying to turn back the Yaquis but neglected maintenance due to their extended absence had rendered the wall practically unserviceable, with the adobe crumbling under fallen logs.

Tucson
March 4, 1827

To the acting governor of Occidente, Francisco Iriarte:

On February 23 the Tubac commander advised us that he had just received an official letter from Cananea with news that the Yaquis had attacked that settlement.

At the same time, Chief Antuna, leader of our Apache scouts, got word from Chief José of the Santa Cruz Apache scouts that the same Yaquis were maneuvering to attack Tucson. Then, once they have penetrated our district, they will ally with the Coyotero Apaches, Papagos, and Yumas, who plague us during most of the months of the year.

In the face of this threat—and since we now have no troops here—I called an emergency meeting immediately here at my house. We must first do something about the presidio wall, which has fallen down in many places.

In a spirit of unity, and with admirable patriotism, all agreed to begin at once making adobes and securing timbers to restore our military wall to its original strength. I beg Your Excellency's commendation of the outstanding willingness and harmony of these settlers. I have seen it every day since the departure of our troops, and I am seeing it right now in the matter of the wall. At a moment's notice they promptly leave their work in their fields to chase the raiding Apaches.

Juan Romero [rubric]

6

Manuel Escalante Defends Tucson

1828

The terrifying expectations expressed in Juan Romero's report in March 1827, our preceding document, were softened by the Yaqui peace treaty of April 13, signed at Potam between Jusacamea and José Figueroa. Tucson's problems, however, were not over.

The weakness of the Tucson presidio, including its very structure, was observed not only by Juan Romero (March 4, 1827) but also by Apaches from the White Mountains, Tucson's traditional foes. In the spring of the following year, there descended on the Santa Cruz Valley the unheard of number of nearly a hundred Apache warriors (routine raiding parties usually consisted of seven or eight). Their primary target was the mining operation in the Sierrita de Oro Mountains a few miles southwest of Tucson. They besieged the area in mid-April, leaving a number of miners dead, and went on to steal an entire herd of cattle west of Tucson on April 17.

Between the Yaqui threat of 1827 and the mass Apache attacks of 1828 — in addition to other problems, which our document outlines — the Tucson area seemed to be living in ever-increasing danger. In early autumn of the discouraging year of 1828, the civilian population of Tucson held a town meeting and voted unanimously to leave the area to the military and move en masse to a safer area of Sonora. As an even stronger reason to move, they gave the decline of the presidial military economy.

Tucson was in the Arizpe political department, the head of which was Manuel Escalante, who had known Tucson well since the beginning of the century, which he describes as the golden age of the Old Pueblo. His epic report, besides securing help from the state government to reverse the

settlers' decision to abandon the town, informs us of important events in
Tucson history that appear in no other source. Manuel Escalante was a
giant in the history of Sonora under early independent Mexico and later
would become independent Sonora's first constitutional governor.

Arizpe Department
December 9, 1828

To José María Gaxiola, Governor of Occidente:

I must apologize for not answering until now your letter of October 24, in which you solicit my comment on the report from the mayor of Tucson (Ignacio Sardina) concerning the plight of the settlers there. Two urgent trips on horseback, one to the Moctezuma district and another to the Pima mission at San Ignacio, have occupied all my time. Since the Tucson situation is so critical, my love for its settlers and my familiarity with its situation prompt me to make my recommendations to Your Excellency immediately without seeking further information directly from Tucson.

It is well known that Tucson is the most isolated outpost of our frontier. Despite constant vigilance, the civilian settlers there are unable to guard their livestock and other possessions from Apache rapacity. Not one of its citizens has been able to count even twenty-five head of cattle in his herd even though our Arizpe department is famous for the abundance of its cattle. If a Tucson settler is able to call one or another horse his own, it is because of the permanent garrison there, which constantly guards the entire horse herd. His bulls and oxen he protects in a pasture during the day, but at night he has to enclose them within the walls of the presidio. This manner of life has finally driven the Tucson settler to the brink of despair.

There are other problems. The Pima settlement on the west bank of the Santa Cruz River, known as El Pueblito, was there before the presidio. For this reason it enjoys Tucson's principal advantage, a magnificent spring of water that gives life to its extensive agricultural lands. Only by virtue of a formal treaty with the Pimas of El Pueblito do the non-Indians on the east bank have a right to one-fourth of this water for the so-called presidio fields.

When I was a frequent visitor in Tucson between 1809 and 1814, the settlers were also farming the Tres Alamos site [on the San Pedro River near modern-day Benson] to provision themselves, the presidio, and the peaceful Apaches attached to the post. Then when Captain Antonio Narbona, their avowed protector, turned over the military command [ca. 1815] to a well-known frontier commandant [Lt. Col. Manuel Ignacio Arvizu], the greater part of Tucson's settlers moved away. This is why at the present time Tucson must depend for its grain supply on the San Ignacio Valley, over a hundred miles to the south.

In previous years the settlers at that isolated presidio of Tucson produced between 2,000 and 2,500 bushels of wheat annually, enough for all their needs. To their eternal credit, this they did with a gun or lance in one hand and a sickle in the other. Many lost their lives supplying the needs of Tucson.

All of this they did even enthusiastically under the aegis of Captain Antonio Narbona, a military commander who fought at their side and for them, as well as understanding both their wants and their worth. In those days Tucson was not only holding its own but progressing, but now the civilian settlers have decided to abandon the post entirely. Things changed radically after Narbona left. Their troops are no longer being paid in money and provisions. The major factor of their decision is certainly the poverty of our military economy, upon which their civilian economy is totally dependent. These, I believe, are the true causes of the complaints and ultimate decision of Tucson's civilian settlers.

I shall now suggest a few remedies that might be applied, for every effort must be made to forestall the abandonment of the magnificent site occupied by Tucson, and its citizens must be encouraged in every way to return once again to the progress they were making in former years.

The first measure that should be taken is to order our state military commander to provide Tucson's civilian settlers with the ammunition they need to defend their strategic position. Only in this way can they put their personal firearms to use and form the local militia that they are authorized.

A second essential requisite for Tucson, more than any other post on our northern frontier, is a local military commander who would rather sleep with his gun than with his wife. At the same time, he should have enough political sense to work along with the civilians, supply their needs, and understand their way of life.

Also, an effort should be made to keep Tucson's professional military post at full authorized strength. The military should be commanded to give first preference to the private enterprise of Tucson's civilians and should be forbidden to look for better prices elsewhere in provisioning their troops with food and other necessities.

The commander, or the quartermaster, should be ordered to make payment for these commodities in one open-market transaction, directly and in full, instead of making partial payments for partial supplies.

The death penalty should be applied to officers guilty of black-market dealings and sharing profits with outside suppliers. The practice of provisioning the Tucson presidio through commissioners here in Arizpe must also be stopped. All of this adds up to the presidio never actually receiving all that it pays for.

Then, some adjustment absolutely must be made in the distribution of water. Tucson's Pima village, El Pueblito, now has few inhabitants. They still, however, have a monopoly on three-fourths of all the water. Legal steps should be taken to award at least half of Tucson's water to the settlers, especially since the Tres Alamos farms, unless I am mistaken, now belong to a private ranch.

Manuel Escalante y Arvizu
[rubric]

7
Armageddon
in the Missions

1828

Although the influence and eloquence of Manuel Escalante in the preceding document staved off the total abandonment of Tucson by its settlers, problems remained — and the principal problem, all agreed, was the basic one of provisioning and sustaining the troops. A professional garrison was essential for what Escalante called "the most isolated outpost of our frontier," and was the rationale for building the presidio at Tucson a half century earlier. Escalante's eloquent attempt to stem corruption in the process of provisioning Tucson's troops was both admirable and necessary but really did not — and politically could not — strike at the heart of the matter.

A delicate economic balance had developed through the centuries between the presidios and the missions. In order to protect the missions, the presidios were generally built as close to them as Indian land rights would allow. The missions returned the favor by selling items from their extensive stores of livestock and foodstuffs to the presidios at reduced cost.

However this stylized arrangement worked in reality, it came to an abrupt and tragic halt in 1828. The beginning of the end of the mission economy of the Pimería Alta had nothing to do with religion, as overzealous defenders of the sacred might surmise, but everything to do with money and politics.

For nearly a decade, Mexico's native-born citizens had been casting an envious eye at the peninsula-born Spaniards living in a Mexico now free and independent of the Iberian Peninsula. The centuries of political superiority of the peninsulars — most of whom had an advantage in business connections with the mother country, land grants, and other favors from the Crown — were now a thing of the past.

Five days before Christmas 1827, the federal congress passed the long-expected Decree of Spanish Expulsion. Except for special circumstances, the decree included all but one of the Franciscan missionaries residing in the Pimería Alta. The state congress of Occidente, then seated at Alamos, followed suit on January 30, 1828. It outdid the federal decree by allowing only thirty days for peninsular Spaniards not exempted by federal decree to leave the state.

The federal decree specifically exempted Spaniards in "necessary posts." Since there could be no necessity greater than the stability of the frontier missions, the Pimería missionaries should have been exempted. The business interests of Culiacán, however, in league with the Occidente politicians, whose state treasury was empty, coveted the Indian properties of the Pimería Alta. Our document reveals their hidden agenda.

Magdalena
November 1, 1828

Observations Classified as Secret Concerning the Missions of the Pimería Alta

The friars continually and consistently impressed upon the Pimas that all mission properties are the legal and rightful possession of the Indians alone. Three centuries of Spanish domination and the degrading and dehumanizing exemptions granted the Indians have made these people incapable of ever accepting our present system of government. They are irremediably prejudiced in favor of monarchy, and their lack of intelligence will always prevent them from understanding anything else.

Proof of this was the reaction of the Pimas of San Xavier del Bac and Tucson to the efforts of Santiago Redondo to stabilize the economy of their missions. If he had not promised them a higher appeal, they would have fled to the Gila River then and there.

At this very moment the native governors of Tubutama and Saric are here in Magdalena complaining against my civil subcommissioners at those mis-

sions and demanding the right to control their own mission properties. I have
had to refer this matter to Manuel Escalante, political chief of this department
of Arizpe. I presume he will keep you informed of further developments.

I am insisting now on only one central administration for the wealth of all
the missions, instead of an individual civil commissioner in each mission, precisely to delay reaction on the part of the Pimas. Only in this way can we gain
time to sell off gradually the effects of these missions. Only in this way can we
ever refill the depleted treasury of our state.

By getting rid of subcommissioners in each mission, we are also rid of pay-
ing their salaries. If the central administrator is a prudent and patient man, the
entire wealth of the missions can be liquidated before the Indians realize it.

Love for Mexico and a sincere desire for peace on the frontier are my only
motives for making these suggestions. In no way do I wish to anticipate the
decisions of our honorable legislature and my superiors.

> Fernando María Grande
> Commissioner General of Pimería
> Alta

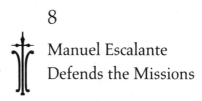

8

Manuel Escalante
Defends the Missions

1830

The initial plans of the ruling powers of Occidente to rape the missions of the Pimería Alta in 1828 were finally foiled in 1830 by Manuel Escalante, the savior of Tucson two years earlier. By the end of 1829, the governor and the commander general who had influenced the state legislature in 1827 to depose the legitimate governor, Francisco Iriarte, and then plotted the despoliation of the missions, had been recalled to Mexico City by the national congress.

This was the event Manuel Escalante was waiting for. He made a tour of all the missions during the two months following Iriarte's reinstatement to assess the situation and then at the beginning of 1830 wrote an appeal to his friend, Francisco Iriarte, who within ten days had returned mission properties to the control of the four Franciscan missionaries named in our document.

Headquarters of the Arizpe Department
January 13, 1830

To Francisco Iriarte, Governor of Occidente:

The missions of the Pimería Alta are situated on the frontier of the political districts of Arizpe and Altar. I visited all of these missions during November and December of last year.

I heard the complaints of the Pimería Alta natives and saw with my own eyes the truth of what they are saying. Before their missions come to complete ruin, I feel an obligation as political superior of these northern districts to change the present system of administering the temporal goods of these missions to the system that made their villages so productive in the past. Your Excellency can consult your own archives for inventories of mission wealth that existed when we expelled the Spanish missionaries two years ago.

Since then, these missions have been administered materially by salaried civil commissioners. Mission property has so disintegrated in the meantime that today there is not enough left to pay one civil commissioner even for a year. The Pimas are in a state of shock.

Your Excellency can hardly be surprised at this. Under the generous aegis of the missionaries, the Pimas had not only a sufficiency for their families but there was more than enough left over for the sick, the needy, and general emergencies. As early as December 1828 I had to hurry to some of the missions to pacify movements of rebellion [see chapter 6]. Under the benign administration of the missionaries, the missionaries themselves provided the Pimas with oxen, plows, axes, and even the seeds to make a decent planting.

Under the new system, many Pimas are leaving their traditional river villages to roam in the open desert with the Papagos. As the Pimas themselves told me: "If the fruit of our labor is no longer our own, it is better for us to leave. If the missionaries no longer administer our villages, soon there will be no villages anyway."

There are only four missionaries left in all of the Pimería Alta. Father José María Pérez Llera, their president, lives at San Ignacio. He attends also to the spiritual care of Imuris, La Mesa, Terrenate, Santa Ana, San Lorenzo, the mission at Magdalena, and all of the surrounding ranchos.

Father Rafael Díaz is at Cocóspera. From there he attends the Santa Cruz presidio, the Tubac presidio, and the missions at Tumacácori, San Xavier del Bac, and Tucson's Pueblito.

Father Juan Maldonado is in charge of Oquitoa, Átil, Santa Teresa, Tubutama, and Saric.

Father Faustino González, an aged and ailing Spaniard, cares for Caborca, Pitiquito, and Bísanig.

I have urged the Pimas themselves to apply immediately to Your Excellency to return the administration of mission property to the few missionaries who are still here and to supply more missionaries for the missions. To this I add my own request for the same purpose: that Your Excellency restore to the four missionaries the mission properties we still have—before the totality of mission wealth is either squandered by the civil commissioners or destroyed by the Apaches.

If these measures are not taken immediately, serious repercussions are inevitable throughout the Pimería Alta.

Manuel Escalante y Arvizu

[rubric]

P.S. I can hardly believe that our American-born missionaries are of less worth than the Spaniards. If the Spanish missionaries, with their prejudice in favor of Spain, administered our missions for us with such success, surely our own can do even better—and with better reason.

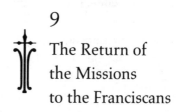

9

The Return of
the Missions
to the Franciscans

1830

Nine days after Escalante's eloquent appeal of January 13, 1830, for the return of Franciscan administration to the coveted missions of the Pimería Alta, Francisco Iriarte, the legitimate and restored governor of Occidente, on January 22 gave both the spiritual and material administration of the missions to the four Franciscan missionaries who were left after the disruptive Spanish Expulsion of 1828.

During the spring of 1830, a very valuable and detailed report on the return of each mission to Fray José María Pérez Llera, the new superior of the Pimería Alta, was made by Fernando Grande, the unscrupulous civil commissioner for all of the missions since July 25, 1828. The excellence of his report perhaps makes up for his earlier chicanery. After all, he was only obeying the orders of Gaxiola and Paredes, who had usurped the offices of governor and military commander of Occidente.

The overall features and minute details for all eight Pimería Alta missions become quite repetitive in Grande's long, drawn-out report. Here we have chosen for publication the section on Mission San Xavier del Bac, the mission nearest Tucson and most familiar to the public.

Cucurpe
May 25, 1830

To the Governor of Occidente:

All Pimería Alta mission property has now been returned by formal inventory to the administration of the friars in keeping with the state decree of January 22 of this year.

These properties had previously been entrusted to me by the decree of July 25, 1828, to forestall the ruin occasioned by the expulsion of the Spanish friars.

Mission San Xavier del Bac

The mission of San Francisco Xavier del Bac lies in a basin formed by two small hills. It is known for its beauty and the fertility of its soil. It suffers from extremes of cold and heat. Its geographical position is thirty-two degrees, thirty-five minutes north latitude and thirty-three degrees, thirty-six minutes west of the Washington meridian. Its satellite mission, some ten miles north, is the Indian village of Tucson, across from a presidio of the same name.

The fields at San Xavier are extensive, and they would all be under cultivation if it were not for the decadence of our presidios, which formerly bought up all of the surplus from mission harvests.

Within the San Xavier mission district, there are two other Indian villages, Santa Ana and Santa Rosa, which flock to San Xavier to help with the harvest, all of which could be much more productive if properly administered. Indian tribes of the Gila River also arrive here in great numbers to pass the frugal winter season, but they return home in the spring.

If, at the present time, this mission could be properly staffed, its many components just mentioned could enjoy a wise, humanistic, and enlightened government.

Since San Xavier lost more than it gained under civil administration, its residence was closed, with all its tools and furnishings inside. Citizens Juan González and Ignacio Sardina oversaw the closing down of all mission operations. Now, however, these tools and furnishings are being handed over to the religious by the native governor, Juan Ignacio Zapata.

Justice is exercised in this village by a representative of the mayor of law and order of Tucson. Both Tucson and San Xavier are in the political district of Arizpe.

Fernando María Grande [rubric]

Affidavit

I, Fray José María Pérez Llera, have received from Fernando Grande the mission of San Xavier del Bac. The mission residence has been closed and the movable goods of the mission stored inside. The key is entrusted to Juan Ignacio Zapata, the native governor.

Fray José María Pérez Llera
[rubric]

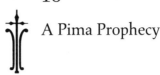

10

A Pima Prophecy

Although the missions of the Pimería Alta were legally returned to the administration of the Franciscans in 1830, the situation of the missions during the following decade would be vastly different than it had been at any time in the more than sixty years of the Franciscan era. Of the eight traditional mission districts, rarely were there more than one or two that had even one missionary in temporary residence. By 1835 the situation had become critical. The native governor of Caborca, years ahead of his time, predicted with amazing accuracy where it was leading. His name was Francisco Neblina, and his family name is well known today in the land of the Tohono O'odham.

Neblina writes also of an Enrique Tejeda, the native captain general of the Papagos, who was paid by the Sonoran state government to lead his people. That role, though now only honorary, is still recognized in the Caborca area.

Written in an even hand by Neblina himself, the original manuscript — over and above its revelations concerning the original mission system — is a tribute to the natives of the Pimería Alta. The Franciscan missionary praised so highly by Neblina was Father Faustino González, a native-born Spaniard. He came to Caborca in 1805, brought the spectacular new church and residence to completion, and dedicated it in May 1809.

Some twenty years later, due to age and infirmity, he escaped the Spanish Expulsion of 1828. All through the 1835 letter, Neblina protects his beloved old missionary and admits he chose a time to write the letter when the old man was away from the mission, lest González's political vulnerability weaken the legitimate Caborca complaints. Fray Faustino lived on until he was well past seventy and died in 1840.

Caborca
February 28, 1835

To the Reverend Father Prefect, Fray José María Pérez Llera:

Since the year 1814, when the Spanish settlers were commanded to look upon us Indians as equals in matters of lands and possessions, we Indians began to lose that filial subjection to our missionary which had been the mainstay of our spiritual and temporal welfare before that time. When the resulting evils became evident and our missionary tried to restore the old order and defend our rights against the encroaching settlers, the new laws of equality were adduced.

Even our Indians who preferred the bare subsistence of roaming in the open desert had recourse to these laws, ignoring the advice of our missionary and resisting the discipline of their own native leaders. When these Indians abandoned their land, our missionary turned those lands over to the paid supervision of settlers, with great loss to our agricultural possessions.

Despite these losses, our missionary secured on credit our clothing and other necessities of life in order to continue the process of our acculturation. The resulting debt was paid off in the following way. Although we needed grain to eat, we gave it to our missionary to sell at a price higher than we could get, and our women—for pay—made *pinole* [a drink] from our wheat. Then, from what he was able to acquire by way of Mass offerings and other donations given him by his non-Indian friends, and from the five bushels of wheat given him traditionally by our Indians in lieu of community labor—plus what was left from the grain sale—our missionary was able to maintain schools in our three villages and care for the widows, the sick, and the neophytes among the baptized, as well as giving something to the unbaptized.

With all of this we somehow continued our temporal and spiritual way of life. Because we remained on our land—and worked it with enthusiasm—the neighboring settlers became fewer and more cooperative. There were always some settlers, however, who tried to stir up opposition from higher superiors—who instead turned out to be our only hope of defense—and our missionary continued to protect us from these threats.

Often we have wanted to go ourselves and present our problems personally before these higher superiors. Our missionary himself, however, has stopped us. Being a Spaniard, he is sure they would blame him for our action.

Wearied by their intrigues, he has for some years now retired from temporal affairs, and we have descended step by step into utter misery. He urges us to be patient and assures us that help will come, but with our Indians at liberty to go wherever they wish and live however they please—some wandering, others working in the mines—and with our own lands owned and occupied by whoever comes along, our villages will become in Indian population like San Ignacio has become—and Saric, Tubutama, and Oquitoa are becoming—and for the same reasons. Even though public safety may be insured by San Ignacio having absolutely no Indians resident there at all anymore, that same public safety will be all the more threatened, as things are going, if settlers take over the four missions mentioned above—Saric, Tubutama, Oquitoa, and finally our own Caborca.

This is because when the desert Papagos have wanted to be baptized, it is in these villages that they have proceeded to settle. These now, however, are the Papagos who are once again wandering about on the desert or are displaced onto ranchos or into the towns of the state—due to the occupation of our lands by settlers and the poverty of our missionary, all leading to our present misery. Were it not for these adverse factors, these villages would now be filled with baptized Papagos—especially in light of their traditional attraction to baptism. Provisioned with the fruit of their harvests—for they are hard workers—they would now be in a position to protect the state against the Apaches and members of their own Papago tribe who prefer to wander in the waterless hills. As it is, however, necessity forces these displaced Papagos to steal cattle and horses from the presidios and the ranchos.

As they wander about the state, robbery and other vices gain momentum as baptized Papagos join together with the desert Papagos, free from the control of mission regulations and free from guidance by their native governors. To increase their forces they even kidnap other Papagos, married or unmarried, gentile or Christian. This type of activity was never seen among our people—or even heard of before their contact with the Yaquis. Now, however, with every trace of their Christian teaching gone, they are becoming as rapacious as the Apaches.

When our missionary dies—and we fear it may be soon because of his advanced age—it may become even more difficult to control our own people [the Pimas] and the Papagos. The missionary that replaces him will not be able to keep us at peace as he has. Also, considering our poverty, we will not be able to support either the new friar or his church, and although Caborca is filled with settlers, they are as poor as we are. Rarely will he be paid for a baptism or burial, with no tithes from the settlers. Even if the new missionary who came could put up with this—and through his own thrift, and help from his friends, be able to give some help to the poorer Indians, the neophytes, and the unbaptized—another father might not. And then if this new missionary might justifiably want us to support him and the church even though we lack the means, then our discontent could result in dire consequences.

Francisco Neblina [rubric]

11

Changes in the
Structure of
Town Government

As the northernmost town of the Mexican federal state of Occidente, Tucson ever since 1825 had been accustomed to local civilian rule by a "mayor of law and order." In our documents we have met a number of them. The situation changed when Sonora was established as an independent state separate from Sinaloa, its occasionally competitive neighbor to the south. Although the federal government officially decreed the separation on October 14, 1830, it was not until the end of 1831 that the Sonoran constituent congress issued "regulations for the internal governing of towns."

The number and nature of the regulations differed according to the size of the town. Tucson was considered a lesser town, since it had less than 3,000 inhabitants. Altar and Arizpe both had more, which entitled them to a town council. The interplay between these three settlements meant that in practice they constituted a historical and political unit. They thought alike, acted alike, and faced common problems.

The decree establishing towns was issued on December 15, 1831, at Hermosillo — for the first time a seat of state government — and the president of the constituent congress was Manuel Escalante, Tucson's special friend. Escalante soon became independent Sonora's first constitutional governor, and for a short time Hermosillo remained the state capital.

Sonoran State Decrees 39 and 40
Constituent Congress of Sonora
Hermosillo, December 15, 1831

Regulations for the Internal Governing of Towns

ARTICLE 39
In all lesser towns there shall be

1. a JUSTICE OF THE PEACE,
2. an ALTERNATE,
3. a TREASURER-ATTORNEY.

In all haciendas and ranchos: an OFFICER OF LAW AND ORDER [*celador*].

Every year on the third Sunday of December the local citizenry shall gather at a place designated to exercise their voting rights and by a simple plurality of votes name the electors (six), who shall in turn elect town officials for the coming year.

In lesser towns the highest local official is the justice of the peace [*juez de paz*]. In all municipal matters, however, he shall coordinate with his treasurer-attorney.

In larger towns, primary obligations will be

1. To test the weights and measures used in the commerce of their municipality against the standard measurements in the state capital. Faulty instruments will be destroyed. Any merchant caught with fraudulent scales or measures shall on the second offense be fined from one to twelve pesos. The fine goes to the common fund.
2. To ensure good quality in the food and drink that citizens of all classes consume, and to drain lagoons, swamps, and other collections of unhealthy water.
3. To establish and visit on a monthly basis primary schools within the township and report on abuses to the state government.
4. To force parents who allow their children to wander indolently about the streets to send their children to school according to their means or educate them and keep them busy at home lest this indolence lead early on to crimes and other disorders.

ARTICLE 40

All town officials mentioned in these regulations shall serve for one year only. They may not be reelected for at least another full year. Their term of office shall begin on January 1.

Officials related by marriage, or by blood within the second degree, may not serve in the same town at the same time.

Only the officers of law and order for haciendas and ranchos may be reelected indefinitely.

12

☦ Apacheland Explodes

Certainly one of the most successful political policies during the three-hundred-year existence of the Spanish colony of New Spain (1521–1821) was the famed Gálvez Peace Policy, launched in 1786 for the northern frontier by Viceroy Bernardo de Gálvez, who himself had served as a young lieutenant on that same frontier. In fact, it eventually became the model on which our modern U.S. Indian reservation system was formed. During Spanish days, members of the peaceful Apache settlements, serving primarily as military auxiliaries of the presidios, enjoyed phenomenal success as long as they had the wealth and authority of the viceroyalty behind them.

The successive governments of the early Independence period, however, including those of the frontier states, had other priorities. The distribution of government rations to peacefully settled Apaches, routine in Spanish days, fell off drastically as the decade of the 1820s progressed. Non-Indian administrators of peaceful settlements clung to the notion (a very dangerous notion indeed) that all the Apaches, who were peaceful at the moment, would soon be tending to their own livestock, raising their own crops, and even sending their children to school.

Although unrest was already brewing in 1831 among the peaceful Sonoran Apache settlements, including those at Tucson, the Chihuahua auxiliaries at the Janos presidio on the border between Sonora and Chihuahua seem to have been the masterminds of the forthcoming rebellion.

Since the Apaches lacked a written language, the document that follows is one of the rare revelations of how they communicated for massive warfare. In this case, information passed all the way from the Southern

Chiricahuas at Janos to the Gila Chiricahuas, the White Mountain people
(then called Coyoteros), the Pinals, and finally south to Tucson to secure
the alliance of Chief Antuna. Grijalva, in this monthly report, seemed not
to realize what was going on, least of all that an invitation from Janos to
join in war had been rejected in Tucson.

Tucson
October 1, 1831

On the twenty-second day of September, an Apache woman arrived from the
Pinal Mountains with a message for our Chief Antuna from Chiquito, war
captain of the Pinal Apaches. Antuna sent two warriors and three women to
make peace with the Pinals.

On the twenty-seventh day of September, the three female emissaries of
our peaceful Apaches returned with the news that the Pinals had killed one of
the two warriors we had sent.

On the twenty-eighth day of September, our other warrior returned to report that he in turn had killed Nagayé, another war captain[1] of the Pinals.

José Grijalva [rubric]

13

✝ The Patriotic Section

In his long career of leading the Apache auxiliaries of Tucson, Chief Antuna never showed any sign of infidelity, including during the long Janos Rebellion. The same negative factors that were influencing Janos, however, were affecting Tucson and the other Sonoran Apache auxiliary settlements. By early 1832, all complimentary rations had been stopped by both the Chihuahuan and Sonoran state military commanders. The move was unjust since the Apache allies richly deserved some recompense for their effective and invaluable services.

Though Antuna tried to control desertions, there were a good number of them. Deserters joined what were unpopularly called the "bronco Apaches." The same scenario was repeated at Santa Cruz, the garrison south of Tucson at the headwaters of the Santa Cruz River. Finally, being attacked and robbed by the peaceful Apache auxiliaries, who had formerly protected them, became too much for the civilian ranchers and farmers. They took the situation into their own hands.

The state military had divided the northern line of Sonoran presidios into a first and a second "section." Copying this terminology, the civilian population on their own created a third section of the northern military line. Appropriately, they christened it the Patriotic Section. It consisted of Tucson, San Xavier, Tumacácori, Cocóspera, Imuris, San Ignacio, Magdalena, Cucurpe, and Tuape.

Fray Rafael Díaz, missionary at Cocóspera, invited volunteers from all the settlements to an organizational meeting at his mission scheduled for the night of May 20, 1832. There was a democratic election for mili-

tary commander of the group, and Joaquín Vicente Elías of the well-known Arizpe family was chosen.

On June 4, Elías, at the head of some two hundred volunteers, entered Arivaipa Canyon from the San Pedro River just south of its juncture with the Gila. They were just in time to surprise another organizational meeting of Chiquito and twenty-five of his Pinal warriors with most of the renegades who had deserted the presidios at Tucson and Santa Cruz. The battle that ensued was one of the most decisive in regional history: within four hours, more than seventy Apaches lay dead in the fastnesses of Arivaipa Canyon, with only one casualty on the Sonoran side.

The document that we translate here was chosen from among many to represent the transcendent significance of the battle and best summarizes the event itself. We suspect that Elías, the elected commander of the group, went directly to Arizpe after the battle. There had been some doubt that the state would authorize the creation of the Patriotic Section, but that could be settled easily now. The state capital had been moved to Arizpe in the meantime, and a special friend of the component towns of the section, Manuel Escalante, was now governor there. Elías reported the battle in detail to Don Manuel, and Escalante thought it significant enough to spread the good news as far away as Chihuahua and its state governor, José Madero. Madero, in turn, thought it significant enough to print Escalante's letter in a Chihuahua government circular, which we translate as follows.

Arizpe
June 27, 1832

To José Isidro Madero, Governor of Chihuahua:

Your Excellency:

Since your jurisdiction of Chihuahua and ours of Sonora are both beleaguered by the cruel and indomitable Apaches, we feel we should share the good news of any advantage we gain over them. Besides, we have always treated one another as neighbors and brothers in the republic we support together.

In Arivaipa Canyon on the fourth day of the present month, a force of some two hundred of our citizen volunteers engaged our common enemy on their own ground. After a relentless and valiant attack that lasted all of four hours, our citizens proclaimed a complete victory. Seventy-one Apache warriors lay dead on the field. Thirteen under-age captives were taken. Two hundred and sixteen horses and mules were recovered.

God and Liberty!
Manuel Escalante y Arvizu

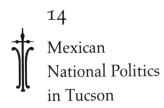

14

Mexican National Politics in Tucson

1834

*From Spanish times, the frontier presidial system had depended on the viceroyalty and Mexico City, not on provincial governors, for every phase of its support. Shortly after the fiscal intendency and the commandancy general for the northern line were established in Arizpe in 1776, a royal pay station (*pagaduría real*) was attached. The pay station was subject only to a royal intendant and was, once again, quite independent of provincial or local government. The royal intendant system was part of the Bourbon reforms inherited from the Sun King, Richelieu, and seventeenth-century France and was designed to modernize imperial administration and to end provincial corruption.*

*From this pagaduría, with its close royal connections, the presidial soldiers received their wage (*prest*), and the frontier missionaries received their stipend (*sínodo*). Once a month it was an important day in Tucson when the paymaster of the presidio (the *habilitado*) set out with his protective escort to begin the monthly ride to Arizpe to get the company payroll.*

With the advent of the republic, federalism worked best for presidial and mission representation and gave more power to the frontier states to support their own presidios. In fact, federalism became a kind of traditional preference for frontier towns, including Arizpe, precisely because of the importance of the military presidios in the area.

There was, however, a split among the federalists in Mexico City in the early 1830s. Ultraliberal federalists were campaigning against the very concept of a professional military, the lifeblood of the presidial system. The Tucson pronouncement that follows was prophetic. Within four days, Antonio López de Santa Anna would take over Mexico City and move the nation toward centralism.

Tucson
April 20, 1834

THE JUSTICE OF THE PEACE of the Tucson settlement pronounces in favor of the plan proposed by the settlers at Santa Cruz five days ago. Following this plan and the compelling motives behind it, we change our obedience from the sovereign congress of this state and proclaim our allegiance directly to the central government of our nation.

We see this as the only way to restore the status of our professional presidial troops and save this state from total destruction at the hands of the Apaches. As it is now, the funds necessary for the maintenance of our presidial troops are being used solely for the support of the state congress and its useless agencies, with absolutely no benefit to the public. A general meeting was held by our local citizens. They agreed unanimously that the entire length of our frontier is collapsing. Our presidios are not being funded, and the livelihood of our civilian settlers likewise depends on this funding.

> Juan González
> In the name of all citizens of
> Tucson

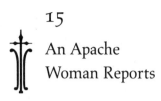

15

An Apache
Woman Reports

On July 3, 1834, the Sonoran legislature at Arizpe finally authorized
Governor Manuel Escalante to organize the massive offensive against the
Apaches that the frontier had awaited for five years. In 1829 the state of
Occidente had formally decided upon a strictly defensive posture until
the depleted state treasury recovered, which it never did until after the
division of the state in 1830.

Coincidentally, just as the offensive was being approved in Arizpe, an
informant in Tucson provided information of great importance to the
coming campaign in the document that follows. Our informant is an
Apache woman. We do not know her name, only that she belonged to the
peaceful Tucson Apache settlement. She acquired her invaluable knowledge while spending three months as a captive of the principal group of
rebel Apaches from both the Chihuahuan and Sonoran presidios.

Tucson
July 3, 1834

To José María González, Adjutant Inspector of the Northern Line:

Last evening one of our Apache captains, Bautista by name, brought in the
Tucson Apache woman who was taken captive in the March 30 raid on the

Babocómari rancho by a band of bronco warriors who had deserted their presidial posts. Later she secured a horse and was able to escape when the warriors left for a raiding campaign while their families went out to gather agave.

She admitted that she had little hope of finding her own peaceful band, since an Apache named Matías, who recently ran away from the Fronteras presidio, told her falsely that her band had been betrayed and that those not killed by Mexican treachery had joined the rebels.

For this reason, she came down to the Santa Cruz River seven days ago. Staying close to the mountains and under cover of night, she searched for her own band. Finally she discovered their trail backtracking eastward to the Ciénega de los Pimas, where they often camped. Not finding them there, she followed their trail northward around the west end of the Rincón Mountains. In the sierra of Santa Catarina [i.e., the Santa Catalina Mountains] among the saguaro forests of Sabino Canyon,[1] she found evidence that her people had gathered saguaro fruit there. Now she knew that Matías had lied to her.

So she came on into Tucson to join her people. Once safe here at home, she felt free to give important information concerning the whereabouts and activities of the rebel bands who had deserted our presidios.

She learned from her captors that they are living—and even sowing crops—in the Mogollón Mountains. About half of the rebels had come south with their families to gather agave in the Chiricahua Mountains, which they are using as a base camp for their raids. They then send the stolen horses, mules, cattle, and sheep on up to the Mogollón settlement.

She claims they are planning an early attack on Tubac and Santa Cruz. Although she does not know exactly when, she warns us that they will certainly come in great numbers. They have not yet joined up with the Pinal and White Mountain bands, but from the time she was taken captive she heard that these two numerous bands have been planning a massive raiding campaign. Meanwhile, the rebels are gathering agave in the Chiricahua Mountains while they wait for the two larger bands to come south and join them. She also revealed that the rebels are getting their lead and gunpowder from the Santa Rita del Cobre mines in exchange for stolen mules.[2]

Ensign Loreto Ramírez

16

✝ Tubac Undefended

In the following letter, Juan Bautista Elías, Tubac's justice of the peace in 1834, describes the plight of Tubac during early Mexican times.[1] The occasion was his report to Governor Manuel Escalante on news received from the Tucson presidio of an imminent attack on Tubac by the Apache auxiliaries who had deserted their presidios. Some Apaches were gathering agave in the Chiricahua Mountains of what is now southeast Arizona for future raiding expeditions, while the main body was in the Mogollón Mountains of southwestern New Mexico. The rumor was related by the Apache woman informant in our preceding document.

Tubac
July 4, 1834

To Manuel Escalante at Arizpe:

Your Excellency is very familiar with our area and our situation, how our dwellings are scattered out among the arroyos and undergrowth, our presidio is without a wall, and worst of all how the winter rains have changed the course of our river, placing our water almost beyond reach, especially if we are under siege by the enemy Apaches.

We have not even one artillery piece to defend us in such an event. Our few settlers are nowhere near adequately armed, and our professional military, upon whom we can depend only if our paymaster returns, consists at most of ten or twelve armed men.

The enemy Apaches are fully informed, never fear, that Tucson and Santa Cruz are protected by their presidial walls, their artillery pieces, their generous complement of well-armed settlers, and their authorized number of professional troops. The Apache will think twice before attacking them but will give no thought at all before attacking Tubac.

I enclose a copy of the circular sent out from Tucson yesterday, warning us of imminent attack. If this should indeed come to pass, Your Excellency may rest assured that this settlement of Tubac will cease to exist within a few hours.

Juan Bautista Elías [rubric]

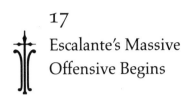

17
Escalante's Massive Offensive Begins

1834

The Sonoran state legislature at Arizpe approved Governor Manuel Es-
calante's plan for an all-out counteroffensive against the presidial Apache
rebels on July 3, 1834. Escalante established what he called his "campaign
division headquarters" at the Babocómari rancho, on the very edge of the
Apache heartland. Still an active ranch today, the Babocómari, beside the
San Pedro River, lies on the northern boundary of the Fort Huachuca
military reservation. The boldness of Manuel Escalante's strategy and the
number of men he put into the field were never matched in all of Spanish
and Mexican times. As to the apprehensions at Tubac, the Apaches were
masters at the art of bluffing, and Manuel Escalante knew it. There was
no attack on Tubac.

The next document presents Manuel Escalante's first extant com-
munication from his newly established headquarters on the Babocómari.
He is writing to his vice-governor back at Arizpe, reporting in late Sep-
tember on the extensive campaign preparations he had conducted since
obtaining approval from the state legislature on July 3.

Campaign Division Headquarters on the Babocómari
September 29, 1834

The Vice-Governor of Sonora at Arizpe, José Ignacio Bustamante

Your Excellency:
After some difficulty in securing Indian allies for the campaign, two days
ago I was able to launch our first detachment, which will remain in the field

for twenty-four days. Antonio Narbona and Ramón Urrea are the general commanders for these six companies of cavalry and infantry, 442 men in all.

Over and above these 442, more than a hundred troopers are still here with me guarding 200 loads of provisions and 1,800 replacement mounts. Once the fighting force has advanced sufficiently, I shall move the supplies and horse herd forward to La Playa de los Pimas.[1]

Today I am sending word to Tucson to supply me with a complement of Papago auxiliaries, and to Santa Cruz and the San Ignacio Valley that I am now ready to receive the men they have recruited. I thought it best to launch my first detachment as soon as possible, to make room for the components of my second detachment, which is more seasoned and will compensate for the mistakes of the first.

The mountain ranges between the San Pedro River here and the Mogollón Mountains in New Mexico, particularly the Chiricahuas, must be scoured for renegades before we meet their main force in the Mogollón Mountains.

I am sending no word of my activities to the New Mexico and Chihuahua authorities until I am completely sure of my own operation.[2] Would you kindly inform those authorities for me as soon as you receive word of the success of the second stage of my plan—namely, launching my second detachment from La Playa de los Pimas and advancing my supply train to San Simón?[3]

Manuel Escalante y Arvizu
[rubric]

18

✟ Victory in the
Mogollóns

*Based once again on the invaluable early July information of the Tucson
Apache woman that the renegades gathering agave in the Chiricahua
Mountains were waiting for the Pinals in the north to come down and
join them, Escalante authorized Juan González, justice of the peace in
Tucson, as early as August 19, to form an independent detachment of
twenty-seven settlers, ten Pima allies from San Xavier and El Pueblito,
and twenty Apache scouts. They left Tucson on September 16, added 200
Papagos, including some Gila Pimas, at the Gila River, and then penetrated the Pinal heartland as far as the Salt River.*

*The Pinals were taken by surprise. Never had their country been in-
vaded so deeply. If there had been plans to team up with renegades in the
Chiricahua Mountains, they were now forgotten, thanks to the foresight
of Escalante and Juan González. The Tucson detachment returned home
on October 1, four days before Escalante launched his elite force, three
hundred cavalry and infantry drawn mostly from the San Ignacio and
Santa Cruz valleys, directly at the renegades in the Mogollón Mountains.*

*On October 20, with their twenty-four days in the field completed,
the first detachment returned to division headquarters. By this time Escalante had moved his command post some twenty-five miles southeast
of the Babocómari to the better accommodations of the hacienda of San
Pedro, just south of where the international border crosses the San Pedro
River today. From this date forward, the San Pedro hacienda would become a permanent military outpost, manned by federal troops rotating
out of the San Pedro presidio.*

Our main focus in the Mogollón drama is the second detachment,

which left the Playa de los Pimas on October 4. The long journey to Mo-
gollón took twenty days. Avoiding mountains, and broken ground gen-
erally, they favored the lower desert route—for the same reasons, we must
conclude, that it is favored by our modern interstate highway, plus the
safety of open ground. It also explains why Escalante destined his supply
train for a final position at San Simón, along this same route.

Moving eastward across the continental divide, they must have pa-
tronized Ojo de Vaca (Cow Springs), a perennial watering place for
expeditions traveling through southwestern New Mexico. Here they sur-
prisingly changed course, wheeling their horses back toward the north-
west and the Mogollón Mountains, fifty miles away.

This roundabout route avoided the mountainous approach from the
southwest, where the detachment could be easily ambushed, to say noth-
ing of meeting up with bronco Apache bands distinct from the rebels.
Perhaps more important, the rebels anticipated no danger from the south-
east and Santa Rita del Cobre, a friendly direction.

As they passed down the Mangas Valley, they could already see di-
rectly ahead the peaks of the Mogollón Mountains rising nearly 11,000
feet into the air. The final destination of their long journey was close at
hand. And now, as they rode out onto the plains below the lofty Mogol-
lóns, our document takes up the narrative. It is from the pen of Escalante,
quoting directly from the description given him by his commander in the
field, whom he never names.

The Hacienda of San Pedro
Campaign Division Headquarters
November 2, 1834

In his communication of October 30, the commander of my second detachment
reported to me as follows:

About four o'clock on the afternoon of October 24, the treacherous Tutijé,
general of the Janeros[1] and of all the rebel warriors, and Víbora—also from
Chihuahua—rode with their numerous following out of the Mogollón Mountains to meet us. Maintaining an advantageous elevated position, they did

their best to distract us while a throng of rebel warriors surreptitiously moved to our rear.

We immediately launched a direct charge, our infantry straight up the middle and our cavalry mopping up on both sides. Disregarding the threat from behind, we charged directly up the slope of Apache advantage. These are the brave men, Your Excellency, that I have the honor to command.[2]

We were able to kill only two of them and wound a few others, and to their discredit they left their great captain, Tutijé, our prisoner.[3] We were also able to recover some saddled horses and lances. When the warriors trying to encircle us saw the effect of our frontal attack, they also scattered up into the rocks, where they knew our horses could not follow.

According to testimony later given by Tutijé, we had been spotted three days before our arrival here by members of his band who were out hunting. With this knowledge they were able to send their families up into the mountains farther north.

Today we begin our journey homeward. Our horses are spent, and the twenty-four-day limit to our provisions was passed two days ago. Because of the distance to your hacienda, we must petition Your Excellency to send us remounts and provisions as soon as possible.

[no signature]
As related by
Manuel Escalante [rubric]

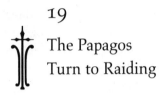

19

The Papagos
Turn to Raiding

1835

Less than two months later, the satisfaction resulting from the success of
Escalante's Apache campaign was dampened by a report from the Altar
district of an unprecedented encounter between Mexican ranchers and
Papago horse thieves. Three Papagos were killed, but they had been the
first to shoot, plunging this traditionally peaceful tribe into ten years of
war. It, and all the reasons for it, had been foretold in the document in-
cluded in chapter 10, "A Pima Prophecy."

As early as February 1835, the theft of an entire horse herd was re-
ported to the Altar authorities. The details and more are revealed in our
document.

Ayuntamiento [Town Council] of Altar
March 4, 1835

To Manuel Escalante, Governor of Sonora:

In their communication of December 31, 1834, our predecessors, the outgo-
ing ayuntamiento, reported to Your Excellency how three of our citizens—
Francisco Monreal, Joaquín Almazán, and Antonio Reina—had killed three
Papago Indians. The three Papagos had stolen some of Monreal's horses. When

Monreal and his two companions caught up with them, the Indians rejected all attempts at peaceful parley. Instead, and without provocation, they opened fire on our three citizens. In the skirmish that followed, the three Papagos were killed. Now, ten days ago, José García reported that the desert Papagos stole his entire horse herd, including his broodmares. We have subsequently decided to send one hundred men under the command of Diego Celaya to accompany García on the trail of his stolen herd.

They tracked the raiding party to the foot of the Quijotoa Mountains.[1] Finding a Papago village nearby, they prevailed upon the local governor to act as mediator to help us recover the stolen herd. Four of our party accompanied the governor into the mountains to parley.

The reply of the raiders was that for the time being the horses must stay where they are, but the herd would be maintained and protected until the three Altareños who killed the three Papagos should be bound over to them for execution. Then the horse herd would be returned intact. The governor and our four emissaries retreated to a water hole to discuss the matter. The rest of our troops waited in another canyon nearby.

Suddenly one of the raiders appeared at the water hole and, feigning friendship, warned us that the other raiders, and many of them, were already blocking the exit to our canyon to kill us and then kill our entire troop. At this point the governor admitted that they had threatened him as well, because of his intervention. He confirmed the claim of the informant that the raiders were indeed many and that we should leave for our own sake.

Celaya and his troops rode into Altar today—with no captives and no horse herd.

Antonio Urrea [rubric]

20

Tucson Makes Peace
with the Pinal Apaches

1836

So much has been made of the rebellion of the presidial Apaches of 1832–34 that our history books have left us with the exaggerated impression that there were no Apache auxiliaries left in any of the presidios of the line, including Tucson.

The Apaches at Tucson, especially Chief Antuna, would have laughed heartily at the notion. Why? Because in July 1835 a census of Tucson Apaches was taken. Still presided over by Chief Antuna and his primary war-captains, Nichuy and Flaco, there were 106 men, 117 women, and 263 children. These families were still receiving wheat rations as in the days of Spanish control. The great length of the complete census, with all warriors mentioned by name, make it impossible to include it here.

The following document, however, may help dispel the popular notion that Sonorans never made peace treaties with Apaches. The largest peace parley ever held between Tucson and its perennial enemies, the Pinal Apaches, took place at the Tucson presidio on March 5, 1836. The fourteen Pinals present also spoke for six other Pinal war captains. The commander general of the northern line, Colonel José María Elías González, presided.

Most surprising of all, it was the Pinals themselves who were asking for the treaty. They could not forget the two worst massacres in their history: that at Arivaipa Canyon and a second that resulted from a Tucson civilian offensive against them that was intended to keep them out of the Mogollón affair. Now the Janeros were trying to implicate them again in revenge for the Sonoran execution of Tutijé and his two Chihuahua Apache companions. The Pinals had suddenly become loyal Sonorans.

Presidio de San Agustín del Tucson
March 5, 1836

On this day at the presidio of Tucson a meeting took place in the temporary residence of the commander general of the department,[1] Colonel José María Elías González. Representing the Pinal Apaches at the meeting were the two Pinal war chiefs, Navicaje and Quiquiyatle; and the Pinal warriors Cadaquil, Esquidare, Pahule, Fraile, Cuchil, Codagostle, Nadijechile, Nagadaije, Alquinante, Ysachide, Estlogue, and Esquinachite. Also present as observers were the Tonto war chiefs Tutugodyafe and Tuquidine, representing also the war chief Bocancha.

The Pinals declared that they are here for the sole purpose of seeking a stable and enduring peace. After a long discussion, they all agreed to the following arrangement:

1. That they submit themselves to the government of the Mexican nation and promise to observe its laws.
2. That, as a consequence, no Mexican troop will attack them, just as no troop has attacked them since they asked for peace.
3. That they pledge themselves as allies of our troops against all aggressors even though those be their own neighbors, the Tonto or White Mountain nations.
4. That they agree to return any female captives to us provided we return two already captured Apaches to them, one captured by the Gila Pimas and the second a captive presently at Nacámeri in central Sonora.
5. That they promise not to make peace with other nations, the Janeros particularly, without previous consent of the Mexican government.
6. That they agree not to harm any Mexican citizen.
7. That no Apache travel farther south than Tucson without a passport from the Tucson commander, to be issued to no more than four or five Apaches at any one time.
8. That for the time being they settle at the juncture of the Arivaipa arroyo and the San Pedro River, or later at another place with the approval of the Tucson commander. Obeying these conditions, they are to be provided with the rations

supplied to other peaceful Apaches and the tools and oxen necessary to cultivate the earth.

9. That every two weeks they report to the Tucson commandant on occurrences in their region, particularly any advance signs of hostile attack.

10. That the door remain open for the further peace treaties already requested by the Tonto and White Mountain nations. To accomplish this, those nations must declare the number of warriors, women, and children in their bands and arrange with the Tucson commander for their place of settlement.

> Signatures: fourteen crosses
> Loreto Ramírez
> José Sáenz Rico
> Antonio Comadurán
> José María Martínez
> José María Elías González

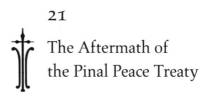

21

The Aftermath of the Pinal Peace Treaty

1837

Faithful to Article 9 of Tucson's peace treaty with the Pinals of March 5, 1836, the Pinal Apaches on January 28, 1837, dutifully reported on the subversive activities of the Janeros to Lt. Col. José María Martínez, commander of both the Tucson presidio and the second section of the northern line between 1836 and 1838. For those three years—as our document reveals—Captain Antonio Comadurán, Tucson's regular commander, was temporarily commanding the presidio at Santa Cruz.

Through our document, Martínez passes the valuable Pinal information on to the commander general at Arizpe, José María Elías González. Fortunately, most of the Janeros' threats were bluffs, and the Sonoran bands they invited to the fray betrayed them to the Tucson presidio.

Tucson
February 6, 1837

To Colonel José María Elías González at Arizpe:

Three Pinal Apaches reported to me on January 28 that they had been paid a visit by a war chief of the White Mountain nation who had a message for the Tucson presidio.

A Janos war captain and four of his cousins had recently visited the White Mountains, revealing a plan for another rebellion. The Janeros were only waiting to harvest a crop. They would send their families to safety with provisions from the harvest and then stage a raid on Sonora. They have vowed to avenge the death of three of their leaders: Tutijé and a second war chief put to death at Fronteras plus a third, Cabezón, killed at Santa Cruz.

The Janeros plan to pitch a tent just outside the gates of the presidio at Fronteras. The local commander and yourself as commander general will be invited to a peace parley in the tent. There they plan to kill you both—there where Tutijé, their general, was imprisoned.

Cabezón, the Janos war captain executed at Santa Cruz, had a son who did not return to Janos to settle in peace after the rebellion. And now, through his influence, some 800 warriors are pledged to help him avenge the death of his father. They plan to sweep on to Santa Cruz—after obtaining vengeance at Fronteras—surprise the Santa Cruz garrison and kill Captain Comadurán, and then go on to Tucson to do away with the peaceful Apaches here, since our Apaches here had been chosen to guard and escort Tutijé and the two other Janos captains from the Mogollón Mountains to their imprisonment at Fronteras.

José María Martínez [rubric]

22

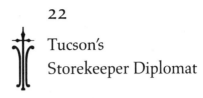

Tucson's
Storekeeper Diplomat

1837

Teodoro Ramírez, son of a pioneer frontier family, was prominent in Tucson affairs from Mexican Independence well into the American period. Here he reports to Sonora's governor, Rafael Elías González, on his own private diplomacy to retain the loyalty of the Gila River nations to Tucson and the Mexican nation. The report contains some grizzly aspects that may be offensive to some readers and involves some diplomatic contradictions, which are explained later.

Elías González passed the Ramírez report, along with an important covering letter, to the minister of the interior in Mexico City. The covering letter — included here following the Ramírez document — refers to Ramírez's diplomacy as a bulwark against an expected invasion by the United States, which would have come as quite a surprise as early as 1837.

Tucson
September 6, 1837

To Rafael Elías González, Interim Governor of Sonora:

Chief Azul of the Gila Pimas rode into Tucson a while back, bringing fifteen pairs of Apache ears. Our presidial commander reneged on his promise to give him a suit of clothes for every Pima campaign he leads against the Apaches.[1]

Azul then proceeded to my house to air his disappointment. His warriors have nine firearms, but not one cartridge would the commandant give him. Even our armorer refused to repair some of Azul's weapons that needed attention.

I urged Azul to continue the valuable service the Gila Pimas have always given us in repelling the Apaches. I also promised to bring this whole matter to the attention of Your Excellency.

On my own I rewarded Azul and his four companions with a change of clothing, some knives, handkerchiefs, a bottle of distilled spirits, and a dress for Azul's wife. They were, of course, quite pleased.

Finally, I turned over to them the fifteen cartridges I had in return for their promise to launch a new campaign once their horses were rested. They were then to report the success of the campaign to me so that I might relay the message to Your Excellency in order to reward them properly for their services.

A few days after returning to the Gila, Azul and Antonio—chief of the Maricopas—conducted a campaign that killed five Apache warriors. They sent me the five pairs of Apache ears with the plea that Your Excellency send them more firearms and ammunition.

More recently, a band of dissident Apaches stole some forty oxen and cows from the presidio. With some difficulty I organized a private posse to give chase and at my own expense sent two dispatches to Azul together with nine packages of cartridges, one for each of his riflemen. To recover our herd, Azul responded with a pledge of warriors not only from the Gila villages but from the Papago country as well. I shall report to Your Excellency as soon as they return from the stock recovery campaign. Our loyal allies on the Gila should be rewarded at state expense with firearms and ammunition, bolts of broadcloth, and suits of clothes for their leaders.

With encouragement, the services of the Gila Pimas might be extended beyond containing a few dissident raiding bands north of us to staging an effective offensive against our true enemies to the east, the Janeros. For my part, I intend to encourage them in light of my duty as a patriotic citizen. It is my hope that other private citizens along our frontier may follow my example, including an organization of civilian volunteers to participate actively in their offensive. I pledge my personal services to such an organizational effort.

Teodoro Ramírez [rubric]

Arizpe
September 20, 1837

To the Mexican minister of the interior:

The accompanying copy of a letter from Teodoro Ramírez, a Tucson merchant, should impel the president of our republic to authorize the expenditures requested.

In the light of current events in Texas, the United States of America has already as much as declared a state of war between our two nations. The populous nations of the Gila could serve as an important bulwark against the coming invasion.

Rafael Elías González
Provisional Governor of Sonora

An American Fortress
on the Upper Gila

1837

In our preceding document, Rafael Elías González, Sonora's governor, was writing to Mexico City as early as September 1837 of an imminent American invasion of what is now Arizona in light of the Texas Revolution of 1835–36. Such rumors were rife around the middle of the decade. Ramírez, the shopkeeper diplomat whose efforts to preserve Gila Pima loyalty to Tucson are described in our preceding document, popularized the rumor contained in the following narrative.

On a business trip to Arizpe in mid-September 1837, he spread a report — possibly originating with his Gila Pima friends — that about forty Americans were building a fortress on the upper Gila River. The exact site would probably be in the fertile area of modern-day Safford, where the Americans were also farming.

The present and preceding documents might be interpreted as constituting a friendly game of one-upmanship. Lt. Col. Martínez came off rather badly with the Gila Pimas because of his commitment to the Pinal Apache peace treaty, whereas Teodoro Ramírez won the day. In the following report, Martínez testifies — with all due respect to Ramírez — that he knew all about the so-called fortress in July 1836, more than a year before Ramírez spread the sensational rumor in Arizpe.

Tucson
November 4, 1837

To Ignacio Elías González, Commander General of Sonora:

I am writing to you in response to the letter of September 20, which the governor of this department [Manuel Escalante] wrote inquiring into the certainty of the information that Teodoro Ramírez, a Tucson merchant, brought to the capital [Arizpe] concerning certain locations where foreigners, apparently North Americans, have been discovered building a fortress.

I myself first heard this through the Pinaleño Apaches in July 1836. I immediately sent two of my own trusted Apaches up the Gila, the river along which this fort was being built. My emissaries returned on August 8 with the information that they had found some forty Americans at the spot, tending a maize crop they had planted in the area.

The fortress turned out to be a small fortified house outside of which they had mounted a light cannon that they had brought along. While my emissaries were there, the Americans left for their own country. They later came back, bringing others with them. In November of last year [1836] they harvested their crop, moved out, and have not been seen since.[1]

José María Martínez
Commandant at Tucson

24

✝ Greedy Goldseekers and Papago Gold

1838

On March 14, 1838, an extraordinary session of the federalist legislature at Arizpe under the presidency of Manuel Escalante, appointed José Urrea, fresh from the federalist wars in central Mexico, as the new federalist governor of Sonora.

During the very next month Santiago Redondo, political chief of the Altar district, reports to Governor Urrea in the first of our series of documents concerning Papago unrest resulting from the discovery of gold — much to the displeasure of the Papagos — near Quitovac in 1834.[1] Entrepreneurs from the centers of wealth in Sonora and Sinaloa of course had great plans for the Papago goldfields, including building a seaport at Puerto Peñasco. Urrea's hometown, Tucson, as always placed Papago loyalty first, as we shall see in the peace settlement of 1843.

Here we translate Redondo's two letters to Urrea, dated respectively April 28 and May 12, 1838, both from Altar. The second contains excerpts from the campaign diary of Rafael Moraga featuring the eloquent words of Tónolic,[2] the prominent Papago leader who defended the honor of his people. His address to Moraga and the Mexican troops reflects Papago nobility and wisdom at their best.

Altar
April 28, 1838

To José Urrea, Federalist Governor of Sonora:

It is a well-known fact that for some years now we have been threatened by the possibility of a Papago uprising due to the discovery of gold in their land. Citizens from every part of the state are now working these mines and investing in them. Reports of new discoveries arrive every day.

It is equally well known that for an even longer time the Papagos have tried to keep the presence of gold in their land secret lest Mexican goldseekers come and take their lands away from them.

For example, when a Quitovac Papago first discovered gold at nearby San Antonio, he did everything in his power to mislead Mexican inquirers, leading them down all kinds of blind alleys. Finally, our own experts had to find the San Antonio site by themselves.

Apart from numerous reports, I myself have been eyewitness to Papago discontent in such villages as Quitovac, Sonoita, Carricito, Soñi, Arivaipa, and Cubó. This is totally understandable in light of the insults and even extortions they have suffered at the hands of unscrupulous Mexican miners, and also because of the enormous amount of water taken from them to supply the mining camps—particularly in the lands acquired by Diego Celaya, which the Papagos consider as theirs by right of residence there from time immemorial.

There can be no doubt that Papago discontent will increase as more and more water and lands are taken from them. If the Papago revolt feared by the justice at San Perfecto[3]—he wrote to me on April 17—has indeed broken out, Your Excellency now knows its causes and background. I implore Your Excellency to take action against Diego Celaya's illegal occupation of Papago land. This action alone would be a major step toward securing a Papago peace.

Santiago Redondo [rubric]

Altar
May 12, 1838

To José Urrea, Federalist Governor of Sonora:

Together with this letter to Your Excellency, I enclose the original campaign diary of Rafael Moraga, commander of our auxiliary company,[4] which describes his expedition of April 24 through May 1 with sixty of his auxiliaries through the mining camps of the Papaguería.

This expedition was occasioned by a plea for help from Ramón Oviedo, justice of San Perfecto. The danger of a Papago uprising, which Oviedo reported as imminent on April 17, has now been shown to be nonexistent.

As explained in the campaign diary, an incident at Carricito between the Papago governor there and a Mexican miner named Diego Celaya gave rise to this false alarm.

This time we were saved from further incident through the good graces of Tónolic, governor of Cubó[5] and a prominent Papago leader. It is nevertheless quite true that, before and apart from this incident, there has been a general unrest among the Papagos due to our mining activities.

Isolated elements within the tribe itself have been preaching rebellion to the others. I am personally convinced that this is true—until I have definite evidence to the contrary. Papago witnesses at the mining camp of San Hilarión have testified to my conviction. Furthermore, I myself have been an eyewitness to many signs of Papago resentment in my frequent tours through the mining camps.

Moraga confirms this in his diary by pointing out the basic submissiveness of the Papagos to our laws and their love of peace, on the one hand, and individual cases of unrest on the other. Despite this seeming contradiction, we both are convinced that there are many, many good and peaceful Papagos who could never ascribe to a total rebellion, and thus it is our founded hope that these will dissuade the others from doing harm.

Santiago Redondo [rubric]

The following is an excerpt from Rafael Moraga's campaign diary enclosed with Redondo's letter.

April 27, 1838

On this day we arrived at the settlement of Soñi.[6] Here I was met by Tónolic, the Papago governor of Cubó, and the governors of Carricito, Ayoma, and Tac, all accompanied by constables, alcaldes, and other officials of their government. After each of us greeted one another individually, I commanded my troop to dismount and adjourned the meeting to my place of residence.

Tónolic came along presently and through my interpreter, Miguel Mendoza, a retired lieutenant, offered me twenty of his men to take our horses out to pasture and water. My first temptation, of course, was to refuse the offer, since the Papagos vastly outnumbered us. Not counting those who later came with their families to visit us, the warriors who greeted us in our first encounter numbered over two hundred.

After some thought, I accepted Tónolic's offer to care for our horses in order to prove to his people that we had not come to fight but instead to urge them to accept public peace and order.

Giving orders to my ranking sergeant to count the horses and turn them over to Tónolic's men, I immediately turned the conversation through my interpreter to the topic of a possible Papago revolt. Tónolic immediately commented that he knew as well as I did not only of such a possibility but also of the compelling reasons behind that possibility. Nevertheless, he continued, he for one would never think of turning this possibility into actuality.

Many Papagos were not formally Christians, he explained, but they all knew that God had created them and had suffered for them, and they also knew that there was a loving Mother who intercedes with her Son for all living beings.

Papagos believe that all men are one and, even though Papago skins are darker, that God loves them equally with all the others and cares for them despite their offenses against Him, for they know that God does not want them to steal from or do harm to their fellow man. Papagos feel guilty when they do so.

Papagos also believe, Tónolic continued, that God placed many good things on this earth so that all creatures may survive, not just a few. He created the stars in the heavens to set forth His grandeur and power.

On this particular land he created the Papagos. For their survival He endowed it with resources. He also willed that this land not be taken from them. Against those who might try, the Papagos still should not wish to make war.

At this point I interrupted Tónolic and through Francisco Carro, our state-appointed captain general of the Papagos, tried to make him understand that there are legal procedures he can follow when others try to steal Papago lands. Most important, these procedures would avoid armed invasions to seek out dissident Papagos and even enlist the powerful aid of our state governor against the enemies of the Papagos.

Tónolic assured me that he was aware of all of this. For that very reason he was here today. He had even been at Caborca when they began recruiting for my present force. When he asked where these troops were going, they told him that his own nation was rising in rebellion. He told them plainly that this was a lie, because if it were true, he would know about it.

When they told him that some Mexican miners were even leaving their camps on foot, he hastened to San Perfecto. When Ramón Oviedo, the Mexican justice there, told him the same thing, Tónolic begged him not to believe any more rumors of revolt because he and his people were planning no such thing. He swore that he himself would go out and settle this whole matter, and if there were any truth at all to the rumors, that he would personally come and report to Oviedo.

Tónolic then hurried on to his own village [Gu Vo] and from there began to gather the governors and other native officials that he has brought here. It was the Carricito governor who finally explained to him how the rumor of revolt had started.

Diego Celaya had appeared at Carricito one day with orders from Oviedo at San Perfecto to clean out the village well and dig it deeper in order to fill the water carts supplying water to the mines and also to accommodate the livestock the Mexican miners were pasturing there.[7] Celaya had brought along the necessary tools, nine workers, and also an interpreter. The Carricito governor and his people also offered to help the Mexicans.

It was at this point that Celaya made the fatal proposal to use the dirt taken out of the water hole to build a dam to restrict all water coming into the area to this one well. The Papago governor tried to reason with Celaya that this would dry up all of the water holes used by the Papagos in the area. Celaya now grew angry and tried to continue his harmful project by force. The Papago governor grabbed him, threw away his crowbar, and pushed him away from the water hole.

When Celaya left, the governor turned to the workers and invited them to join him in faithfully carrying out the direct orders of the Mexican justice at San Perfecto. Oviedo, not Celaya, represented Mexican authority in their region. In this way, both Mexicans and Papagos alike might freely share in the water, which they do to the present day.

Celaya now went to San Perfecto. There he falsely reported that the Papagos had impeded him by force of arms from cleaning out the well, and this false report was the sum total of the rumored Papago revolt. . . .

Rafael Moraga

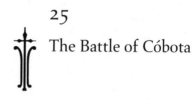

25

The Battle of Cóbota

Despite improved relations between the Altar political district and the Papaguería through the diplomacy of Tónolic and the patience of Santiago Redondo in 1838, raids on Mexican cattle continued. By 1840 it was well known that the principal source of these raids was the so-called Tecolote district, most of which is still within the Tohono O'odham reservation in the United States. In 1840, however, the fortresslike village of Cóbota in the Cóbota hills south of the present border, dominated the district, since it served the district dwellers both as a refuge for stolen cattle and as a defense against pursuing Mexican ranchers.

Dionisio González had also replaced Santiago Redondo as prefect of the Altar prefecture.[1] Papago distrust and suspicion were matched only by González's lack of diplomacy. Judging from Rafael Moraga's successful performance with Tónolic two years before, the battle of Cóbota might have been avoided had Moraga been in full charge.

On May 11, 1840, 150 Altar auxiliaries clashed with more than a hundred Papagos near Cóbota in the Tecolote district of the Papaguería. One Mexican and twelve Papagos were killed.

Cóbota battlefield
May 11, 1840

Diary of Operations to Pacify and Restore Law and Order in the Tecolote District of the Papaguería

Under orders from Dionisio González, political chief of this Altar district, with twenty-five of my men I approached the concentration of Papagos who were perched on a spur of the Cóbota hills. Our laudable purpose was to offer the Tecolote leaders yet another chance to accept peace and public law and order. Their warriors, however, immediately answered my overtures with bullets and lances.

I now noticed that the hills were covered with many more Papagos than I had seen at first. The circle of warriors were joining their leaders in the hills. I began my offensive, therefore, by chasing as many as I could up into the higher reaches of the crags to render their fire less effective. I counted at least three dead Papagos in the course of this maneuver. I had no time to look for more, since even from the heights they were still wounding some of my men. I then pulled back toward the center of the field.

Since my small detachment had nearly used up its ammunition and also needed water, I ordered a retreat to the halfway point, where our larger force was waiting by the water hole. I kept an eye out to see if the enemy would try to follow us. This would be my chance to retaliate.

After about half an hour at the water hole, I gave orders for the entire force to remount. We then began a march to the rear from the halfway point between the two camps. I stayed with the rear guard, hoping that the Papagos would follow. We had gone a little over half a mile when 100 Tecolote warriors suddenly appeared not only behind our rear guard but on our flanks as well.

We stood our ground, forming a square with our total force. I ordered a section of our rear guard to dismount and operate as infantry. When the Papagos saw that at their sudden appearance we did not run, they began to move back. Before they could get away, I ordered the infantry to charge, protected on both sides by the cavalry. Our cavalry lances alone took seven Papago lives. After the battle I counted nine Papagos dead, which together with three killed on our charge up the hill, came to twelve in all. Counting the multitude of their wounded carried off on horseback in their escape, I must now consider the Tecoloteros duly castigated.

In calling the roll and reconnoitering the battlefield, I discovered only one of my force gravely wounded. I just received word at this time of writing— about four o'clock—that he has died.

I have eight more wounded in noble parts of their bodies. They will heal.

Rafael Moraga

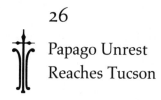

26

Papago Unrest
Reaches Tucson

1842

In late November 1842 a violent conflict broke out within the very walls of Tucson's presidio between desert Papagos and Tucson's peaceful Apaches over a misunderstanding about stolen horses. Captain Antonio Comadurán, the presidial commander, came to the rescue and averted what could have become a major incident. In our document he explains the causes of the misunderstanding and describes in full detail the subsequent events.

Tucson
December 1, 1842

To Colonel José María Elías González, Commander
of the Northern Line:

About three o'clock yesterday afternoon, the governors of the Papago villages of Santa Ana, Santa Rosa, and Lojia came in to see me. A good number of their people accompanied them, including some from the rebellious Tecolote region. Each one of them was armed. Somehow they got past the outer guards by slipping through openings in the presidial walls.

Arriving at my place of residence, they immediately laid their complaints before me. Our peaceful Apaches, according to this Papago delegation, had stolen fourteen horses from the village at San Xavier del Bac. The San Xavier villagers followed their tracks and interpreted a concentration of tracks in the Sierra de la Madera[1] as the site where our peaceful Apaches had met a group of bronco Apaches and—all according to previous arrangement—had turned the horses over to them. The Papagos claimed to have then followed the tracks of our peaceful Apaches here to the presidio. I believe, however, that the whole Papago story is a misinterpretation of something that happened some days ago and that I was fully aware of.

Five of our peaceful Apaches went hunting for deer in the aforementioned mountains. While there, they spied two horses hobbled in a box canyon. They went over to them and recognized that they had been left there by bronco Apaches, who then went on to raid in the area of our settlements. Nearby they also found two cinches and gear for a harness hanging from a tree, together with a sack of fresh horse meat. They brought all of these items here to the presidio to show them to me.

On the day following the arrival of the two hunters here, the same bronco Apaches raided San Xavier and, for obvious reasons, retreated through the same mountains where they had left the two horses hobbled and the harness gear hanging from a tree. This accounts for the tracks that the Papagos correctly identified but then proceeded to misinterpret the activity they represented.

I explained all of this in detail to the Papagos. When I saw that they did not accept my explanation, I even offered to go with them to the site, accompanied by the five Apache hunters and a troop escort. If the Papagos could prove their version of the story, I would proceed legally against my peaceful Apaches and make them return the stolen property. Since the Papagos came armed and with intent to take justice into their own hands, as soon as they heard my just proposal they ran from the presidio straight toward our peaceful Apache settlement, which lies outside the presidio walls.

Just as they were about to launch their attack, I caught up with them and ran unarmed between them and the Apache camp, shouting for the Papagos to calm down. They hesitated only a moment and then pushed forward—knocking me down—to try to butcher my peaceful Apaches, who refused to fight back.[2] In the confusion I was able to get far enough away from the fracas to shout the order to sound a general alarm. Both troopers and settlers flocked to the scene. On their way they observed Papagos in the cornfields hurling lances at the Apaches trying to get away.

As soon as my troops opened fire, the entire Papago force turned and fled toward San Xavier. Although no one was hurt on either side, the Papagos were able to make off with some of the horses of our peaceful Apaches, shouting back that our troopers and settlers were nothing but a pack of coyotes.

The Papago governors who appeared here armed yesterday came in today unarmed. They returned the horses they had taken from the peaceful Apaches. I lectured them on the seriousness of their offense. They admitted their guilt and knelt down before me to beg pardon for the disorder they had caused at my presidio. I immediately accepted their apology but warned them that we could not be as patient with them next time.

Under no condition should they ever enter this presidio armed. If they failed to leave all weapons at El Pueblito upon their arrival here on whatever business, I would have to treat them as enemies. They left the presidio today, promising to mend their ways.

Despite the happy ending to this story, yesterday's series of events spells potential danger to this presidio. There is a distinct possibility of an alliance of all the Papago villages to avenge real or imagined wrongs on our part. The representation here yesterday of villages farther to the southwest, which are already in rebellion, makes this danger even more real. In fact, rumor has it that yesterday's entire incident was prompted by an attempt on the part of the aforementioned rebellious villages to win over to their side the friendly villages nearer to us.

This leads me to my final point, a plea that your commandancy general make every effort to send us more men and supplies. We need armament above all, since our few settlers simply do not have the weapons to help us resist the possible Papago rebellion mentioned above, and the other companies of the sector of the line under my command certainly have no men to spare.

God and Liberty!
Antonio Comadurán

✝ Quitovac under Siege

1842

Captain Antonio Comadurán, the author of the preceding document, had spent well over twenty years in close connection with the Tucson presidio, most of that time as its commander. His prediction on December 1, 1842, of the potential spread of the Papago problem came true within two weeks. On December 14 rebellious Papagos laid siege to the principal mining center of Quitovac. In the following document, the subprefecture's political chief at Altar, Lorenzo Martínez, describes the concurrent events, including the civilian evacuation of both San Perfecto, a very active Mexican mining center prominent in our previous documents, and Quitovac itself.

The report of Lorenzo Martínez embodies the very apex of the ten-year Papago War. Addressed to General José Urrea, it is also the first of our documents to introduce another important political change in the supreme government of the Sonora department near the beginning of 1842. The year before, Urrea's forces in Durango had backed General Santa Anna, who overthrew Anastasio Bustamante's bid for the presidency. In return, Santa Anna appointed Urrea to replace Manuel María Gándara as Sonora's civil governor and military commander general on February 9, 1842.

Gándara again started what amounted to a civil war, only this time more viciously. Sonora never really forgave Gándara for his unscrupulous methods. He began by inciting the Yaquis to indiscriminate attacks. Less than two months after Urrea took office on June 1, Hermosillo itself was attacked, on July 24, by more than 600 Yaquis. Gándara also sent subversive emissaries as far north as the Gila River to make attractive

*overtures to the already rebellious Papagos. It was not until November 24
that Urrea temporarily defeated the Gandaristas at Opodepe, northeast of
Hermosillo. Apart from the harm done by the Gándara rebellion itself, it
kept Urrea from attending to other important matters, such as the Papago
situation, for much too long a time. It was not until April 1843 that he
was finally able to launch an adequate offensive against them.*

Subprefecture of Altar
December 21, 1842

To General José Urrea, Governor and Commander General
of the Department of Sonora:

For too long now the Papagos have been molesting the towns and ranchos of
our Altar political district. We have been powerless to punish their continuous
thievery, for two reasons: our lack of military forces and our fear of a chain
reaction that might once again stir up the revolutionaries on the Yaqui delta.

The documents I herewith enclose should bring Your Excellency up to date
on the seriousness of the situation at present, including in recent weeks two
hundred head of cattle stolen and the mines of Quitovac besieged. Quitovac
and other mining settlements of our district have simply not been able to maintain an armed force adequate to insure the safety of their settlers. Nor are these
settlers, as they themselves have told me, about to punish Papago thievery, for
fear of the sure reprisals openly threatened by the Papago nation.

With the concurrence of the military commander of this presidio, we have
assembled a military force strong enough to cover a safe retreat of the settlers
from both Quitovac and San Perfecto to Altar. When these towns were under
siege on the 14th and 15th of this month, this force was not as yet organized.
Our military commander has now sent out a detachment of 100 armed men,
together with a mule train, to bring in these settlers and their possessions.

Even with this operation in progress, the Papagos at this very moment are
still raiding ranchos and carrying off whatever their hearts desire. Nor should
we ignore the source whence springs this rebellion.[1] Although there is no

doubt that the Papagos are in communication with the Yaquis, the Papagos have no other immediate interest than thievery.

Today we received unofficial word that the Yaqui rebellion has been put down, which gives me all the more reason to hope that Your Excellency, free now of the Yaqui disturbance, can now employ the most energetic measures to quell this Papago revolt. We have treated them with the utmost consideration, but this policy has failed, and we totally lack resources to carry on the full-scale war that they have unilaterally declared.

Although our Altar subprefecture is in turn under the prefecture of Horcasitas, in this emergency I have bypassed that headquarters. We want Your Excellency to know our situation and act as soon as possible to remedy it.

God and Liberty!
Lorenzo Martínez

28

Tucson Girds
for Defense

1843

Antonio Comadurán, veteran commander of the Tucson presidio, wrote three letters in early March 1843, included here, to report on the alarming extent of native unrest throughout Sonora stirred up in conjunction with the western Papago revolt. Comadurán also mentioned the seditious involvement of Manuel María Gándara in the process. Gándara was even having some success in inciting rebellion among the peaceful peoples of the Gila for the first time in the long history of Spain and Mexico in the Sonoran Desert.

Comadurán did not know that only the day before, on March 4, the Sonoran governor, General José Urrea, had issued a circular to all the settlements of Sonora calling on them to contribute men and arms for a massive offensive to end the Papago War, which had dragged on since December 1834. General Urrea, related by blood to both Comadurán and Elías González,[1] was not only a family member of the far frontier presidial society, being born in Tucson itself, but was also known nationally as a military genius through his involvement in the fight for federalism and in the Texas War.

Tucson
March 5, 1843

To the commander of the Northern Line, Colonel José María Elías González, at Rayón:

An undercover investigation was conducted by the civilian justice of the peace of Tucson into the subversive plans of the friendly nations of the Gila River, in conjunction with the Papago rebels of the west, to attack these presidios of the frontier. There is no doubt that there is some such plan afoot among these tribes, spurred on by the success of western Papago plundering. This incentive is magnified by the attractive invitation of an emissary of Manuel Gándara, who claims to be on his way from the Yaqui River with the entire Yaqui nation to take over our settlement and put an end to our people.

The general of the Gila Pimas, Culo Azul, accompanied by the general of the Maricopas, Antonio, paid me a visit yesterday to profess their loyalty to this presidio. To test this loyalty, the rebels are indeed running stolen stock up to the Gila under the guise of trade.

Azul informed me during his visit yesterday that when he refused to take part in this activity, many of his villages revoked their obedience to him; also that these are the same villages that are openly admitting that Manuel Gándara is behind all of this with his tempting promises and that they have even been visited by Gándara's personal representative, an Indian from Horcasitas named Sósthenes [*sic*].[2]

Azul has steadfastly refused to endanger the welfare of his entire nation through involvement in these political maneuvers, continues his dedication to agriculture, and as far as bearing arms is concerned, has restricted himself to his traditional alliance with us against our common enemy, the Apaches. Antonio of the Maricopas said substantially the same thing.

After listening to their lengthy testimony, I, too, lectured for some time on the advantages of peace and the danger of subversive collaboration, whereupon they asked me to draw up a document attesting to their loyalty, which they in turn could present personally to the commander of any punitive expedition sent against them. I supplied them with two such documents.

On the basis of their testimony, I am now convinced that certain segments of their tribes have declared open and total warfare and that all of our frontier garrisons will soon be under attack. I am therefore appealing directly to your office as commander of the presidial line, since our governor and commander general is fully occupied with the southern sedition of the Gándara brothers.

Could you at least send us, as soon as possible, as many lances as you can, one light cannon, and 50 firearms with corresponding ammunition in order to arm our settlers and our peaceful Apaches for a defensive stand? Our scarcity of horses makes an offensive campaign impossible. At the moment I am strengthening our fortifications and calling in our peaceful Apaches, who are away right now gathering mezcal and attending to pursuits relating to their sustenance. With these measures and the requested emergency supplies from you, I am confident we can hold out until your superior office dictates further orders.

> God and Liberty!
> Antonio Comadurán

To accompany his official report, Comadurán sent the following private communication.

Tucson
March 5, 1843

To my esteemed relative and friend, José María Elías González:

It is always with a certain diffidence that I write official letters. I hope, therefore, you will not take it amiss if I add this second letter to convey my personal opinion on how to react to the hostility of the western Papagos, especially in light of the scarcity of water facing any invading troop from here.

We must concentrate our forces here at Tucson to control and influence the rapidly increasing numbers of western Papagos who are fleeing the war zone to settle at Tubac, Santa Cruz, and as far south as the Magdalena Valley. Some measures must be taken immediately to counteract the influence of rebellious elements of the Gila tribes, who are already disquieting these refugees with messages of threat if they do not join the uprising immediately.

Tucson also has an easier and better-watered access to a greater part of the Papagos. In conjunction with the forces from Altar, we could more effectively control most of the Papaguería. At the same time, we can block the Gila peoples from corrupting the western Papagos who have fled to the Santa Cruz Valley and beyond.

I have just arrived from a trip to Arizpe, where I was able to secure only two carbines, two measures of powder, and two slabs of lead. Nor could your adjutant inspector there spare me any infantrymen. This is why I am appealing directly to you in my accompanying letter for the 50 firearms, ammunition, and one light cannon.

On the last leg of our return journey from Arizpe, I received a bulletin from my Tucson presidio of such distressing content that I feared the enemy might intercept my pitiable escort and myself and relieve us of even the few armaments we were able to secure from Arizpe.

With only one aide, I rode ahead under cover of night in order to send out a larger force to insure the safe arrival of my escort. This enabled me to meet sooner with the Gila generals who were waiting for me here. I hoped through them perhaps to win more time for your superior office to take the necessary action in this matter.

With this personal note I send you my fondest greetings. I hope that you will command imperiously this your friend and relative, who attentively kisses your hand.

Antonio Comadurán

Tucson
March 12, 1843

To Colonel José María Elías González:

On March 10 a Papago suspect was apprehended here in Tucson's El Pueblito. I had him brought to me at once. He was officially accused by Juan Yorem,[3] a resident of El Pueblito, of being one of the Papagos sowing discord up on the

Gila. The suspect swore that he had come in only to attend a scalp dance at San Xavier del Bac celebrating the killing of an enemy Apache by the people of that village.[4] Since he refused to say more, I sent him to jail.

The next day he sent word to me that he was ready to tell me what I wanted to know. I sent for him and assured him that I knew all about the planned uprising and exactly which villages were involved.

He replied that although the purpose of his visit really was the scalp dance, as he had told me the night before, he also knew that the Gila villages and others of the Papaguería were now taking active part in the western revolt. There were exceptions, he added. Culo Azul with some of his people, and Antonio, general of the Maricopas, with some of his, together with the Papagos camped at Tubac, Santa Cruz, and along the Magdalena River, who had fled there with their families to avoid revolutionary involvement, all refused to rebel.

Outside of these exceptions, everyone who remained in their villages were with the revolt. As proof, all of the villages without exception took part—he among them—in the attack on Oquitoa, where they killed some people, sacked the church, and stole some cattle and horses, which they divided up among the villages.[5]

Since then, there has been a continuous coming and going of Papago raiding parties under the leadership at various times of Chalan from the Gila River, Saba (whose Piman name is Quiote), Suque (who had been a soldier at Tubac), Juan Ignacio (who had been raised by the settler Quintero at Tubac), and a Christian Papago from the Sauceda village named Sóstomo, also known as Muno.[6]

As a consequence of all of this, I have decided to send a Santa Rosa Papago, who came in with the suspect, to all of the native villages on the way to the Gila. He will present a document—the contents of which have been fully explained to him—assuring the native governors that our government will punish only the guilty. It will urge them to separate themselves from the rebels into a neutral village, where our government will respect them. Otherwise, our invading troops will surely kill them.

I planned to send another document destined only for the Gila villages and requested the Pima governor of El Pueblito to deliver it personally, since he had relatives in those villages. Despite his good faith, however, he declined by reason of delicate health. Afterward, he frankly confided in me that he does not trust those relatives. The interpreter added for him that he would probably feel more at home among the Apaches.

I believe that, with all of this, your superior office will be fully convinced that the Papagos are now in full rebellion and that it could grow even worse if we do not cut it off at the start. As I stand by for your orders and aid in the matter, I am taking every precaution to guard against a surprise attack. Also, I am cautioning the commanders at Tubac and Santa Cruz to keep a close eye on the Papagos arriving there.

God and Liberty!
Antonio Comadurán

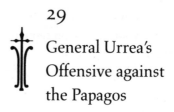

29

General Urrea's Offensive against the Papagos

1843

While Tucson was seriously preparing for an imminent Papago attack, there was much preparation in central Sonora for the great April offensive called for by General Urrea on March 4, 1843. Exactly one month later, on April 4, Lt. Col. Felipe Flores, at the head of a force of some five hundred armed men, marched northward out of the Altar headquarters for a twenty-day campaign against the Papagos. By April 10, Flores had established his base camp in Fresnal Canyon, a spacious, well-watered ravine at the northwest corner of the Baboquívari range. Fresnal Canyon was centrally located to launch forays in six directions through the vast Papaguería. The perennial Papago stronghold of Baboquívari Canyon lay only a few miles to the south. After the campaign had lasted twenty days, the minimum time specified by Urrea, Flores reported to the state's military commander general.

Fresnal del Baboquívari
April 24, 1843

To Colonel José María Elías González:

I left Altar on April 4 and arrived here at Fresnal on April 10, following various trails of stolen stock. I know I am being observed by the enemy because when

I took command of my present position they sent up smoke signals all through the Baboquívari Mountains.

That same afternoon they came down to skirmish on the desert floor. When our cavalry charged, they fled as usual. By observing their retreat that afternoon, I observed their principal position to be in Baboquívari Canyon.

I made a reconnaissance of their stronghold and gave orders immediately to 300 men under Lt. Col. José María Martínez to occupy the heights behind and surrounding their canyon during the night. During the same night I took up a position at the mouth of their canyon, leaving a respectable force behind to guard our headquarters and supplies.

When day broke, all of our forces were in position. Some fifty warriors came out to do battle. Hilarión Gálvez, an Indian from Pitiquito, was wounded in this action while rounding up some stolen stock in the canyon. Due to the rocky terrain, the enemy escaped, but we discovered the remains of their camp, from which they had evacuated their families prior to the battle. So we returned to our headquarters and supplies, bringing with us the stolen property we had recovered.

On April 14, I set out with a force of 150 men to follow another trail of stolen stock that led in the direction of a mountain known as Bandak [Coyote Well].[1] There we came upon eight warriors still driving the stolen stock, which we recovered. We captured a warrior wounded in the encounter we had had with them. We also took a woman and three children prisoner. I ordered the warrior shot on the spot as an example to his fellow brigands. The next day we returned to Fresnal with the recovered stock.

This made a total, to date, of 278 head of cattle we have recovered. Their various original owners took possession of them and then returned home. Eighty-one horses and mules had also been recaptured, some of which were pressed into service for the campaign.

On April 19, I set out with the entire expedition for the west toward Artesa Well.[2] The water was so scarce there that I had to send Lt. Col. Antonio Urrea,[3] most of the troops, and the supply caravan back to Fresnal Canyon.

With a force of 150 men I continued on from the Artesa Hills toward the Cababi Mountains where, according to the trail we were following, there was an enemy gathering.[4] And so there was.

Around one o'clock on the afternoon of April 20 we clashed with some forty-five warriors who came out to meet us. Four of them were killed in the encounter. In the cavalry chase, directed by Ensign Lorenzo Rodríguez, two more died. Another woman with three children was taken prisoner, and more stolen stock was recovered.

On our side, Charles Grimes—a foreigner who had been acting as surgeon for the expedition—was wounded and died two days later.[5] Esteban Quiroz, a volunteer, and Juan Ortiz, ensign of the Oquitoa auxiliaries, were also seriously wounded.

I recommend that your superior office give very special recognition to Ensign Lorenzo Rodríguez,[6] who led thirty of our cavalrymen for some fifteen miles in the successful cavalry chase following the encounter at Cababi. Due to the weariness of the horses, he was not able to overtake the Papago families who had gone ahead of the warriors.

I myself followed him on that chase, leaving orders for Lt. Col. José María Martínez to follow us with the rest of the troops. They joined up with us during the night, and the next day we all returned to the water at Cababi. From there we returned here to Fresnal Canyon and our supplies.

I also recommend for your recognition our three wounded men and the entire troop led by Ensign Rodríguez, who comported themselves heroically from the first moment of the encounter until they were unable to inflict further punishment on the enemy due to darkness, the roughness of the terrain, and the weariness of the horses. The thirst they suffered during this lengthy action was extreme, and we all shared that thirst until the next day.

I assure you, sir, that these regions are practically impassable because of the scarcity of water. Despite all this, we will renew our march on the morrow toward Quitovac and Sonoita on the basis of information gathered from our most recent captive, and experts who accompany me, that there may be sizable Papago gatherings there.

This is all I have to report to you to date, sir, so that you in turn can relay this news to His Excellency the Governor and Commander General of the Department of Sonora. I pledge to you my sincere admiration and respect.

God and Liberty!
Felipe Flores

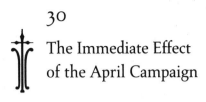

30
The Immediate Effect
of the April Campaign

1843

Toward the end of April, Comadurán at Tucson had sent a personal emissary, Carlos Castro, to Culo Azul on the Gila River. Castro bore an offer of amnesty from General Urrea himself—if Azul could gather all of the Papago leaders and bring them to Tucson for a peace parley. The April offensive of 1843 made so great an impression on the Papagos that it is recounted to this day in Tohono O'odham oral history. Carlos Castro returned to Tucson on May 3 with the best of news.

The letter presented here is from Manuel Orozco, retired ensign of the Tucson presidio. It reached Comadurán on his way to Santa Cruz to discuss plans with the commander there, Lt. Col. Francisco Narbona.

Tucson
May 3, 1843

To the commander of the Tucson presidio,
Captain Antonio Comadurán:

Carlos Castro has just returned from the Gila River. There he met with Culo Azul, general of the Gila Pimas, and explained in great detail the contents of your official letter. After a long conversation, Azul agreed to come here to Tucson in compliance with the wishes of our governor and commander general.

He assured me that rebels and nonrebels from every corner of the Papaguería are now seeking refuge with him on the Gila and are pleading for his intervention with our government. After this long conversation, Azul sent messages to all of the river villages to come to him immediately. In a very short time we were surrounded by an immense crowd, which included the refugees from the Papaguería. After the message in your letter was explained to them, the governors of all of the villages with great simplicity expressed repentance for their past actions.

Then Azul consulted with his people about the proposed trip to Tucson. It was decided that first they would have to go on a retaliatory campaign against the Apaches, who had recently attacked them and had killed one of the Maricopa women. Then they could come to Tucson to fulfill their promise. Antonio, general of the Maricopas, fully agreed with all that had been said and assured me that all of the Gila villages were now at peace. One of the rebel governors revealed that he was holding a Mexican woman captive but that he would personally conduct her to Tucson in exchange for his two sons whom we are holding captive.

On the way to the Gila, Castro had stopped at the Papago village of Kohatk,[1] where he explained his mission and where he was well received. The people there assured him that they themselves were at peace but that the rebels, showing signs of sadness and shame, had passed through their village on the way to the Gila to sue for pardon through the Pima general, Culo Azul. Out of fear for our campaign, they themselves were about to collect their families and retire to the Gila. They begged me not to consider them as enemies. Everywhere there was fear that our campaign might penetrate even farther into their land.

Without further delay, I now pass this information on to you.

God and Liberty!
Manuel Orozco

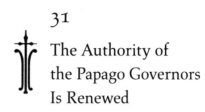

31

The Authority of
the Papago Governors
Is Renewed

1843

Felipe Flores drew up a final peace treaty shortly after May 11, when he was ordered to proceed with 250 of his men to Tucson to ensure law and order during the peace talks. A subsequent letter written during the following year revealed that during June 1843 not only was the peace parley held but a joint force composed of the enormous gathering of Papagos and the 250 Mexican troops also waged a joint campaign against the Apaches.[1]

The following news item from El Voto de Sonora, *a newspaper published in Ures, briefly describes the June meeting, and the document that follows it, from two months after the treaty, reveals that the Papagos were not content with a single meeting, however high the level of participation. In fact, Sonoran officials were receiving protestations of loyalty from sectors of the Papaguería for nearly a year after their initial promise of loyalty at the June peace parley. The final and climactic declaration was made personally by Culo Azul in the presence of General Urrea at Guaymas on April 28, 1844. Urrea, in turn, issued the impressive passport to Azul which appears here as our third item.*

El Voto de Sonora, July 27, 1843

The subprefecture of Altar recently reported to the government of the Sonora department that peace now reigns supreme on the Papago frontier. The peace parley at Tucson, presided over by Colonel José María Elías González, commander general of the northern line, has happily brought the Papago rebellion to a final conclusion.

Tucson
August 15, 1843

To Colonel José María Elías González:

Pedro, governor of the Papago village of Santa Rosa, arrived in Tucson today. You will recall that he was commissioned by your office to recover from the western Papago villages properties stolen during the rebellion.[2] He is accompanied by two other governors from previously rebellious villages.

They turned over 4 mules, 2 horses, and 2 burros, assuring me that this was all of the stolen stock they could find. All of the western villages, they added, were now repentant, obedient to our government, and firmly determined never again to believe the lies of political emissaries. All of the villages expressed their gratitude for Urrea's generosity in pardoning them and will forever accept him alone as their true father.

The two governors who came in with Pedro are from the villages of Gácac and Pirigua.[3] Each repeated the protestations made by Pedro and added that two villages had yet to be visited but that they would soon return any stolen stock they would find there.

All three governors expressed their desire to make this presidio their headquarters and requested that, as its commander, I present them once again with the wands of office that they had brought with them and reappoint them as governors of their respective villages. They vowed to respect in the future only those communications channeled through this presidio so as forever to avoid the grief brought upon them recently by lying emissaries from elsewhere.

I in turn assured them of the sincere desire of our government to protect them and help them, especially in view of their change of heart now and good conduct in the future. This pleased them very much.

I then collected their wands of office, which I adorned with new ribbons, and requested that they prepare to receive them in the accustomed fashion.

They immediately knelt down, and as I presented each with his wand I reminded them of their obligations to both their own villages and our government. Each made a profound bow with his head and kissed the wand of office. Their interpreter explained to me that this meant that they would hold my present action forever in sacred memory.[4]

Finally I gave each of the three a certificate of temporary reappointment as village governor. I urgently request that your office issue a certificate of permanent appointment for each as soon as possible so that I can recall the temporary certificates: for Pedro as governor of Santa Rosa, for José as governor of Pirigua, and for Juan Cuate as governor of Gácac. In recognition of the special services of Pedro as your emissary to the western Papago villages, I rewarded him with eight yards of broadcloth.

God and Liberty!
Antonio Comadurán

Passport issued at Guaymas on April 28, 1844 [5]

Passport issued to General Azul of the Papago tribe and the seventy members of his party to proceed to the Gila River, where he has his residence. Let no one obstruct his passage. All citizens and authorities along the way shall give him shelter and hospitality, as is our custom, and in recognition of his many assurances of loyalty and peace.

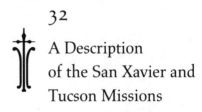

32

A Description
of the San Xavier and
Tucson Missions

1843

The professional restoration work at Mission San Xavier del Bac has attracted national as well as international attention. In 1843, detailed descriptions of the mission at San Xavier and the sub-mission at Tucson were made by the Tucson office of the justice of the peace. A comparison with San Xavier as it stands today is revealing.

In the 1843 report, the interior of the church is described briefly and, minus the wear and tear of a century and a half, seems to have been substantially the same as it is today. It was in the buildings attached to the church and its other surroundings that we find interesting variations.

The Tucson sub-mission, also described in the 1843 report, might be called a satellite of San Xavier, since according to church law it was under the authority of the missionary there. Especially interesting is the detailed description of the purpose and structure of the impressive two-story building that formerly stood on the west bank of the Santa Cruz River near the foot of the black basaltic hill whence Tucson derives its name, the hill known today as Sentinel Peak or "A" Mountain. Many an old-timer remembers the substantial ruins of the building in question. For a time in the last century it was mistakenly thought by incoming easterners to have been an Indian industrial school—perhaps a rather typical response by an industrial New England mentality. Fortunately, our document completely clears up the mystery.

Tucson
May 11, 1843

A Report on the Present Status in Our Region of the Former Lands
and Possessions of the Exiled Jesuits[1]

The San Xavier Mission
The mission of San Francisco Xavier del Bac, some three leagues to the south
of its mission substation here at Tucson, features a magnificent church of burnt
brick and lime mortar. Its construction is said to have cost more than thirty
thousand pesos. It boasts three retablos, one in the sanctuary and, at the tran-
sept, one in each side chapel. The walls of the sanctuary and side chapels are
adorned with oil paintings and full-figured statues of the saints, all of professional workmanship.

Many of the burnt bricks are disintegrating, with the lime mortar washing
out between them, all due to the sudden thunderstorms of summer and the
long, continuing rains of winter. The moisture penetrates to the inside and is
ruining the paintings. If this continues, due to the lack of repair since the religious went away, the whole building will be reduced to a ruin within a very
few years.

The cemetery of the mission has its own chapel, also built of burnt brick.
The chapel door is missing, but the doors of the church are all intact—each
fitted with its own lock.

The mission residence has eleven rooms, two of them of burnt brick, with
all eleven facing an inside square, in turn graced with outer arches enclosing a
covered corridor, also in ruin.

Of the eleven rooms, four are roofed with massive crossbeams supported
by heavy upright timbers. One or the other beam is broken, and as the saguaro
ribs they support are rotting, the entire roof is coming down.

A recreational garden of the religious,[2] surrounded by a wall that is falling
down, boasted a variety of fruit trees, which, through lack of care, no longer
bear fruit.

The communal agricultural lands of the mission are no longer cultivated
and lie barren. Only about an eighth part of these lands and of the garden are
kept up by the native governor. The rest of the planting land is used by the
natives of this village and those of Santa Ana, a remote village subject to the

authority of the missionary at San Xavier. No non-Indians are involved. The majority of even the native residents are without sustenance and unable to farm. This is because of a recent lack of the necessary water, in turn due to neglect of keeping the river water moving and, instead, allowing it to gather in large stagnant pools along the sides.

San Xavier has no cattle and no sheep. The missionary himself[3] rounded them all up and either gave them away or sold them. He even took away the oxen, forcing the natives to plant with a stick or with borrowed oxen. Every year, a few of the mission's wild horses are broken in. These are divided up among the Indians in charge of keeping the fence mended. From within this fence the useless animals are turned loose. It was also from within this fence that the aforementioned missionary took possession of five mules for his own use with no benefit to the mission.

The Tucson Mission

The mission at Tucson, under the jurisdiction and ministry of the missionary at San Xavier del Bac, has a mission church, but its roof is caved in because the supporting beams are either broken or disconnected from their sockets. Other items of wood in its structure have rotted, and its adobe walls have split at many points. Its sacristy and baptistry lack both doors and a roof. All of it can be restored with new wood and a stone buttress. The cemetery, enclosed and with a good gate, is in excellent condition.

The mission residence has seven rooms, all seven opening onto a middle corridor running the length of the building. Above five of these rooms there runs a second story, fronted with an arched and covered balcony. The three rooms on this second floor are used as storerooms.

As elsewhere, the ceiling is threatening to collapse due to rotting saguaro ribs, crossbeams fallen from their sockets, and rainspouts needing replacement. The wood throughout the building is generally in good condition but needs repair in crucial areas that support the ceiling of the ground floor lest these weak spots occasion a complete collapse of the missionary's residence. In one of the aforementioned rooms on the ground floor off the central hall, there is a variety of sacred images, including a crucifix of majestic stature of the miraculous Lord of Esquipulas.[4]

All of the priestly vestments, the sacred vessels, the monstrance, and even the baptismal font were taken to Imuris by the late Fray Rafael. It is still not known how many items he took.

Our native governor sold the door to the sacristy and the door to an upper room of the missionary's residence for a yoke of oxen. The missionary himself sold the door to the baptistry to a settler for a saddletree.

This mission has two gardens for recreation. One is beside the residence. A third of its surrounding wall has fallen down. The second garden, with its arbor and walkway, is larger and has many fruit trees. This garden has no wall, its arbor has disappeared, and its fruit trees are barren. There is a granary some 25 yards long with two aisles down the center to store the grain. It is falling into ruin, with its door ripped off.

The mission agricultural fields, both communal and those apportioned to the Indian families individually, and the plentiful water corresponding, are maintained by only six Indians, who are all that are left. The abundant land left over is farmed by the settlers of this presidio. Since 1840, no rent has been charged for the use of this land, which was opened for public use by the late father Fray Rafael, and at his death his successor, Fray Antonio González.

Before 1840, a rental fee of one bushel for every bushel sown was paid to the mission, as customarily charged by the early missionaries and, after their expulsion in 1828, by those who came after them. Since 1837, however, when the late Fray Rafael began to govern us from Cocóspera and San Ignacio, none of our rental fees have been used for our mission [at Tucson] or the good of the Indians. When he would make his annual visitation, even a much-needed key for the door protecting the room holding the sacred images was not supplied.

From what I have seen personally, 102 bushels were paid for the rental of the lands. He sold some of them at five pesos a bushel and invested the rest in a vineyard he had planted here, only to send the product to San Ignacio. None of this, least of all the removal of the five mules and the *pozole* [soup] cauldrons from San Xavier, resulted in any benefit to the Indians.

As mentioned, the population of the remote Santa Ana mission station, now settled at San Xavier, is about forty families. Although there is an abundance of land to farm at San Xavier, water is lacking. If only a missionary of Propaganda Fide[5] from the Querétaro missionary college could come up and resettle the Santa Ana community at our Tucson mission, where there is plenty of land, and water too! Following the example of the Santa Ana community, many unbaptized Papagos would come in from the desert and settle here, as they did when we had religious from the missionary college of the Holy Cross of Querétaro.[6] Especially since the Tucson people are closest to their cousins to the west and up on the Gila, Tucson should enjoy top priority for a resident missionary. Mission buildings must be repaired and the people instructed in the Christian faith, as was always done in the years before 1828. Actually, since then we have witnessed the reverse. For lack of religious attention, many Indians have abandoned religious practice, left the missions, and returned to the open desert.[7]

I attest to everything in this report as an eyewitness and as well known to others as well. I have thus fully complied with the orders given me.

[no signature]

33

✝ A Final Report on
the Pimería Alta

*Shortly after the ten-year Papago War ended, a much longer story, which
had lasted a full seventy-five years, came to an end: the involvement in
the Pimería Alta of the Franciscans from the missionary College of the
Holy Cross of Querétaro.*

    *During February 1843, we may recall, Comadurán made a journey
from Tucson to Arizpe to seek arms and ammunition to meet the wors-
ening Papago crisis. Roque Ibarra, lieutenant of the Tubac garrison, recorded the presence in Comadurán's party of "Fray Antonio González,
escorted by four civilian settlers."[1] The date was February 8, 1843. The
civilian escort accompanied the friar to the San Ignacio River valley.*

    *Although he was living under the most difficult circumstances imagi-
nable, Fray Antonio stayed on for eight months more, as attested by his
signatures in the baptismal registers, our only guide to his whereabouts.
Due to dwindling personnel, the Queretaran missionary college had formally withdrawn more than two years before, but by legally joining the
Franciscan province of Guadalajara, which still staffed the missions of
eastern Sonora, a persistent Fray Antonio was able to return to ride the
Pimería circuit alone.[2]*

    *Death must have overtaken the valiant friar on one of those circuit
rides or soon after, because some months later the San Ignacio political
district complained of the absence, "since the death of Fray Antonio González," of any missionary in the entire area.[3]*

    *Such was the occasion and significance of the following report, dated
May 2, 1844, on the status of the missions of the Pimería Alta at the end
of the Queretaran period. The author of the report, which had been*

requested by ecclesiastical authority, was the diocesan pastor of the Altar parish, Francisco Xavier Vázquez. As vicario *for all of northern Sonora, it became his task to visit and describe for his bishop the now-abandoned missions of the Pimería Alta. The fruit of Franciscan labors during the previous seventy-five years was much in evidence. The imposing domes and graceful arches made this a sentimental journey for the aging Vázquez. He had known the friars well.*[4]

La Cieneguilla[5]
May 2, 1844

To the Bishop of Sonora and Sinaloa:

A Brief Report on the Indians and Villages They Occupy along the Caborca, Tubutama, and San Ignacio Rivers[6]

The Caborca and Tubutama Rivers

The two satellite missions of Caborca, with Caborca in between, are Bísanig and Pitiquito, administered until now by the Reverend Fathers of the Holy Cross of Querétaro. The Christian Indians of the Caborca mission district face the frontiers of the Yumas of the Colorado River and the gentile Papagos to the north.

Countless numbers of the latter, although they have been catechized and baptized, have fled beyond the frontier. Mexican settlers, lured by the gold and silver mines discovered in Papago territory, have been coming in to replace them. No towns have been established in the mining area, due to the inconstancy of the mines and of the Papagos themselves, who have twice rebelled against the government.

To the east of the Caborca mission villages lies the Altar presidio, now known as La Villa de Guadalupe, with a substantial population. Beyond Altar lie the former missions of Oquitoa, Átil, Tubutama, and Saric. The entire area measures some eighty miles along a curved line from west to northeast.

The churches at Caborca, Pitiquito, and Tubutama are magnificent structures of burnt brick and lime plaster, with domes, arches, and towers, and living quarters joined to the churches.[7] Since the expulsion of the Spanish friars in 1828 and the secularization of the missions, however, the material effects of the missions, including the living quarters, have been impounded. The missionaries have nowhere to live.[8] From the time Your Lordship charged me with their care, I have obediently visited these missions and recovered their living quarters.

The churches are more than adequately furnished with costly vestments, sacred vessels, and all other equipment essential to divine worship. Also, in each mission I have named custodians, with full instructions as to their duties.

The San Ignacio River

In this valley there are eight settlements, with a total population of 5,000 souls, according to a census of four years ago. Three of these eight settlements—Magdalena, San Ignacio, and Cocóspera—have mission churches of the same excellence as those described above and are furnished equally well. The distance from Santa Ana, the southernmost settlement, northward to Cocóspera, which lies up a tributary valley, is more than fifty miles.

Beyond the San Ignacio valley lie the presidios of the Apache frontier: Santa Cruz, Tubac, and Tucson. Their general distance from here is about one hundred and thirty miles. Beyond them live the bloodthirsty Apaches, sacrilegious murderers of Father Alday and a number of other priests.[9]

The mission at Caborca has a library of one hundred volumes, most of them in good condition. At Oquitoa there are 145 volumes, also in good condition. Magdalena, in the San Ignacio Valley, has about the same number. To protect this precious fund of learning, I transferred the books of these missions from the living quarters to the sacristies.[10]

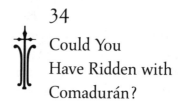

34
Could You Have Ridden with Comadurán?

1844

No other theme recurs more frequently in Tucson's Mexican years than activity relating to Apache aggression. The documentation collected over the last thirty years relating to this theme would burden the reader beyond measure.

By way of compromise, this chapter presents two spectacular and lengthy reports Antonio Comadurán made to his cousin and inspector general of the far northern line, José María Elías González. In them we can follow Captain Comadurán and his Tucson presidials for a full month, from September 5 to October 4, 1844, thereby giving a generous sample of their tireless activity against the aggressive Apaches. The stamina of the Mexican presidial, to say nothing of his Apache foe, finds classic illustration here.

Tucson
September 17, 1844

To Colonel José María Elías González, Inspector of the Frontier:

Around midday of September 5, our peaceful Apaches reported tracks of a large enemy contingent near the Peña Blanca west of here.[1] The enemy was afoot and was headed south toward the interior of the department. The tracks were reported as very fresh, probably made earlier the same day.

By three in the afternoon I was following their trail with a force of fifteen soldiers, twenty settlers, twenty peaceful Apaches, and fifteen Pimas. Brevet Ensign Gerónimo Herrán, acting commander at Tubac, was visiting me here at the time and with my permission joined in the chase. We rode through the better part of the night.

The next day, September 6, at eleven in the morning we took up the trail once again from a place called El Champurrado on the southwest flank of the Sierrita del Oro.[2] We followed the tracks south by southeast across the badlands, riding all day and part of the night.

At noon the next day, September 7, I received word from a section of my infantry, spread out on either side of my cavalry, that they had espied the enemy taking their midday rest in a canyon of the Atascosa Mountains. Immediately I sought out the best trail by which to descend from the sierra above and attack them from the rear. Since I could not get as close as I would like for an ambush, I had to signal the "Santiago" from some distance.[3]

Although we killed two warriors with this attack, the others were able to reach sanctuary in a kind of natural fortress formed by huge rocks.[4] Our cavalry dismounted. Using the high rocks as a shield, we fired on the heights with a rapid volley that lasted nearly two hours. Two more warriors were killed, and three wounded; also, two of our own men suffered minor wounds.

At this point, one of our peaceful Apaches shouted an offer of peace. Their war chief agreed to parley with me if my soldiers would retire to a safe distance. Due to their rock fortress advantage, I was convinced I could do them no more damage despite the valor of my troops. It would only mean casualties for us, and we were low on ammunition. I had brought along only enough for one battle per soldier.

I decided, therefore, to retire my troops to a safe distance and with my interpreter advance to parley with the Apache. He agreed to send his warriors home—they had a good number of wounded—and in proof of his good will to accompany me to Tucson and await the resolution of the commander general as to a peace. For his part, he would do all in his power to influence his people to come to Tucson to settle in peace. I agreed to this arrangement and began to move out with my troops, and he went back to give orders to his warriors.

On the road to Tubac he volunteered important information. As they were leaving their homeland, Quilcedé, another Pinal war chief, was riding out with a force equal to his own, thirty warriors, to raid the central corridor of Sonora all the way to Horcasitas.

When we arrived at Tubac on September 8, I immediately sent word of the other war party south by relay through San Ignacio. We left for Tucson that same day. We arrived there on September 9 at around five in the afternoon, walking our horses because of their extreme fatigue.

On September 11 a cowboy rode into Tucson from the Búsanig rancho in the upper Altar Valley. He broke the alarming news that an Apache war party had stolen sixty horses and mules from the rancho and were making their getaway through the Babocómari rock formation[5] south of Búsanig. I immediately set out to the west with a force of forty troopers, settlers, and peaceful Apaches, arriving at Saucito Mountain on September 12.[6]

There I set up my headquarters to wait for the raiders and to cut off their trail as they came up from the Babocómari along the east side of the Baboquívari range.[7] I waited there until September 15 and on that day headed back toward Tucson.

At eight o'clock on the evening of September 16, I arrived back in Tucson only to hear from Manuel Orozco, the retired ensign in charge of the presidio in my absence, that two days before some Papagos coming down from the Gila had come across tracks of the Apaches I was looking for and of their stolen animals proceeding from the Avra Valley.[8]

In conclusion, allow me to commend the decision and valor of my troops, particularly the Tubac brevet—ensign Sergeant Gerónimo Herrán—who grabbed an Apache warrior by the hair, although a peaceful Apache robbed him of his prey and lanced the enemy to death. I also commend one of my soldiers, Juan Martínez, who killed another warrior.

God and Liberty!
Antonio Comadurán

Tucson
October 4, 1844

To Colonel José María Elías González, Inspector of the Frontier:

On September 29 at eight in the morning, two militiamen from Tubutama arrived here with the news that the Búsanig rancho had been raided a second time by an even larger Apache band, killing eleven settlers, capturing a Mexican woman, and making off with a herd of cattle.[9] The commander of the Tubutama militia, with forty of his men, followed them and was sending word to me to intercept them in case they escaped his pursuit.

By ten o'clock the same morning [September 29], I was riding through the presidio gate at the head of a column of fifty-nine troopers, settlers, and peaceful Apaches. All day long we searched for enemy footprints in the Avra Valley. At seven in the evening we reached the Tortuguitas Mountains on the west side of the Avra Valley with no sign of their trail.[10]

Suspecting that they had long since detected our presence and were driving the cattle northward through the canyons of the Tortuguitas, I sent a detachment into the heart of the mountains and set up a temporary camp to await the report. They were back by eight o'clock, confirming my suspicion that the enemy had indeed moved through a canyon of the Tortuguitas but that the way in was almost impassable.

I immediately chose forty of my men who were in the best condition and sent the rest home. We moved northward down the valley to pick up the enemy trail at the north end of the Tortuguitas. About midnight we finally found the enemy trail. At the very same moment, however, a heavy downpour of rain, which lasted a full hour, severely hampered our operation. Although our horses were miring in the mud, we hurried after the enemy as best we could.

About three in the morning another cloudburst hit us, lasting another good hour. My adjutant, Corporal Solano León, reported that less than ten horses were in any condition to proceed. Nearly all of the force were walking their horses.

Daybreak was near. I knew the enemy was close at hand. Deciding to forge ahead with eight cavalrymen and ten infantry, I gave orders for the rest to follow my trail and do their best to help me in the battle I knew was coming.

On September 30 as day dawned my enemy was in sight on the plain below the Picacho del Gila.[11] Without slowing down our forced march for a moment, we spurred our horses to the attack, my meager force of eighteen against forty-six of the enemy. We soon had them retreating. In the course of a running battle that covered roughly seven miles, we managed to slay two warriors and wound many more—we knew this from the mute testimony of a trail of blood they left behind.

We recaptured the Mexican woman and were able to recover 144 head of cattle, a stolen war chest, four horses—three of them saddled—a mule, and other spoils. The battle ended when the Apaches scattered in the thick underbrush at the foot of the Picacho. We hurried to round up the cattle. It was only then that the rest of the force caught up with us.

The recaptured Mexican woman was the first to tell me of the battle two days before between these Apaches and the Tubutama militia. The Apaches routed the militia, killed five of them, and made off with the war chest we had just recovered. Apache losses had amounted to only one dead and one wounded.

On October 1, I arrived back in Tucson. The Tubutama commander, Benigno Ortiz, was here waiting for me. He confirmed the woman's sad story, adding that besides the five killed, he had four wounded. I returned the cattle, two horses, and one mule to their owner, Francisco García Noriega.

The captive woman was happily reunited with her husband. He had been waiting here in Tucson for news of her. Our presidio kept the three horses belonging to the enemy. Once again let me conclude on a note of highest praise for the endurance and bravery of my troops.

God and Liberty!
Antonio Comadurán

35

Chihuahua Apaches Raid Sonora

1844

In October 1843, in the midst of the Gándara uprising in the south, Sonora was stunned by news of a massive Apache attack and massacre in the region of the Santa Cruz presidio. Thirty troopers and settlers, together with the presidial commander, Lieutenant Manuel Villa, and the presidio's chaplain, Father Francisco Alday, had lost their lives.

When the Boletín Oficial at Ures reported the affair on October 26, 1843, no mention was made of where the raiding Apaches had originated. Later evidence revealed that this and subsequent attacks in northeastern Sonora were being made by the numerous southern Apaches who were receiving rations from Chihuahua authorities at the Janos presidio and who had supposedly settled in peace nearby. Property stolen by them in Sonora was then promptly and openly sold in Chihuahua. One Sonoran commander wryly observed that "the Chihuahua peace treaty with the Apaches" should rather be called " 'Chihuahua's leading industry.' "[1]

By August 1844 the situation had become so intolerable that Colonel José María Elías González, Sonora's commander of the northern line as adjutant for Sonora's commander general, invaded Chihuahua without warning. El Voto de Sonora for September 5 and 12, 1844, reported that his sizable force, collected from various areas of the department, had left Fronteras on August 16 and "has proceeded farther than any of us expected."[2] The observation did not lack a certain tinge of sarcasm. This unprecedented move set off a plethora of correspondence, which we present in its entirety because it clarifies the complex series of events.

November 2, 1844
Fronteras, Sonora
Military Commandancy of Fronteras

To Colonel José María Elías González,
Commander of the Northern Line:

Citizen Teodoro L. de Aros, captain of the permanent cavalry of Altar,[3] responds to the recent request of your superior office for sworn testimony that the Janos Apaches have been raiding in this department and carrying their stolen goods back to Chihuahua to sell.

As acting commander here at Fronteras, I was notified during December 1843 by the justice of the peace at Cuquiárachi that around midnight the night before, the Apaches had attacked that settlement. By the time I arrived there with a force of thirty troopers and settlers, the residents had recovered a young boy kidnapped from the village by the Apaches. During the ransom parley, the villagers had recognized a number of peaceful Apaches from Janos, who taunted them by shouting openly that that was where they were from. I followed the trail of the raiders but lost them when they entered the Sierra del Enmedio, in the jurisdiction of Janos.[4]

Then, on February 7 of this year, an enormous war party attacked the detachment guarding our horse herd less than a mile from the fort. They were able to wound the sergeant in command, gravely wound two soldiers, and make off with more than 200 horses. To make some attempt to recover the herd, I followed them on foot with ten troopers and thirty settlers, which was the only force I had. It was all in vain; there were more than 500 of them.

I was able, however, to set up a ransom parley to recover two young boys belonging to the presidio. Since this parley lasted some six hours, we had every opportunity to deal with their leaders at firsthand. We all recognized Mangas Coloradas, Delgado, Esquinaline, Teboqwuita, Apahe, Chato, Poquito, Juanito, and others known to us by sight—all war chiefs at peace with the Janos presidio. They all held lengthy conversations not just with me but with every member of my party.

On March 5 the same Janos Apaches returned to Fronteras. This time they attacked the settlers working in their fields only thirty paces from the sentry guard. They killed one settler and badly wounded another. I set out after them on foot with my force of only twenty-nine men. The Apaches were waiting to attack me from the heights about a mile away. After some five hours of fighting, they hit me with a bullet that injured my right ear and lodged itself in my skull near the brain. One soldier was killed and two others wounded. During the battle we recognized the enemy as Janos Apaches.

I also know for a fact that the Janos Apaches attacked Cesario Corella's Huépari rancho southeast of here and not only stole thirty of his mules but also stripped the very clothes off his back. During our invasion of Janos territory last August, Cesario saw an Apache walking around the streets of Janos wearing his pants and vest and proceeded to return the favor. On the same occasion I forcibly recovered from Bartolo Samaniego a horse an Apache had sold him from the stolen Fronteras herd.

In the Barranco Colorado, Janos territory, I was eyewitness to the recovery of a herd of cattle recently stolen from Sonora by the Apaches of Janos. When the same Apaches heard we were coming, they fled their village, leaving the cattle behind. We later learned that they had tried to sell the cattle to the settlers at Corralitos. The settlers refused to buy, since the Apaches openly declared that the cattle were stolen from the Villaescusa family of Sonora. This herd is now in the possession of the foreigner "Don Roberto," who will make payment to the owners in Sonora as soon as we contact them.[5]

This, then, is the extent of my firsthand knowledge of the invasion into Sonora and the illegal trade of the Chihuahua Apaches. I respectfully relay it to your superior office in the hope that it will serve your purposes.

God and Liberty!
Teodoro Aros

November 24, 1844
Janos, Chihuahua
Military Commandancy of Janos

To the commander of the Sonoran force presently in my territory:

It is now five o'clock in the afternoon. I have just been informed that a force of some 100 men under your command has forcibly invaded my territory from our neighboring Department of Sonora. I am also told that by way of the

Pacheco rancho, some five miles from here, you proceeded to the settlement at Picacho, also about five miles from here, and there took as your prisoner a faithful Indian named Negislé who, according to my knowledge, was living there with his family, who now in light of your action have fled.[6]

Your strange and shocking procedure is proof positive that you are knowingly violating the rights and laws of this department and, even worse, endangering the harmonious and paternal relations we have with the Indians of our neighboring settlements. Representing our commander general, I must insist that you and your force leave our territory immediately and send Negislé to me in the company of my two soldiers who bear this letter. I shall hold you personally responsible for any consequences that might result from your failure to release Negislé.

I know that you left from Bavispe in pursuit of some Apaches who had stolen livestock from there, but I am mystified that you spurned the honorable victory you might have had over those same Apaches at Álamo Hueco, to which settlement the trail of the stolen stock led.

Instead you came on here to take captive a poor old Apache who can hardly walk and could hardly have done harm to anyone. Furthermore, Negislé has lived here at this presidio for a long time. He left here only fifteen days ago for Picacho to make mezcal. He was coming in every week for his rations.

God and Liberty!
Mariano Rodríguez Rey

November 25, 1844
Tasajera, Chihuahua

To the commander of the presidio at Janos:

How can you be surprised that I have entered your territory when your Apaches cross over to our territory in droves to plunder and kill in Sonora? Then, under the protection of your presidio, they engage in profitable business here, selling the livestock and other wealth they have stolen from us. Allow me to give you a few examples.

On September 26 of this year, Cesario Corella was on his way to Ures with 600 pesos. Near Guásabas your Apache Chichuispe and his raiders attacked Corella's party, wounded one of his servants, and made off with the money. Chichuispe was seen only yesterday at your presidio trafficking with the stolen money and auctioning off the mule that had carried the money and other effects of Cesario Corella.

A few days after the Guásabas attack, the same Chihuahua Apaches— protected by your presidio—assaulted the pack train of Juan Bustamante, killed a woman, wounded three mule skinners, and made off with the mules and their burden. I have traced the stolen goods to the neighborhood of your presidio and can give you evidence of these and other thefts in the following manner. You will notice that I have drawn symbols for a number of livestock brands on the margin of this letter.[7]

My soldiers who bear this letter are bringing a number of items for your inspection. From the property of Juan Bustamante there are a red mule, the brand on which corresponds to the first symbol I have drawn, a cooking pot that his mule skinners had along for use on the journey, and a satchel of tobacco.

From the property of Luis Ramírez, a settler of Guásabas, there is a mare that was stolen around the same time. We were able to catch up to the Apache woman who was leading it. The brand on this mare corresponds to my second symbol. The above evidence should make clear to you that my main interest has nothing to do with "violating the laws of this department."

Then there was the latest raid on the property of Pedro Zosaya, the trail of which I have been currently following. In light of your protestations, I shall proceed no farther on this trail. At the same time, I am hoping that you will send one of your own punitive detachments out to me so that I can point out this trail to them.

One of the trails we followed, from where the raiders divided up the booty and dispersed, led us directly to your "faithful" Negislé, who had in his possession a horse bearing the brand of the Santa Cruz presidio. If my memory serves me right, our Colonel José María Elías González entrusted this same horse to you on the occasion of our first entry into your territory some months ago.

I am also sending for your inspection a roan belonging to Jesús Montaño. Its brand corresponds to my third symbol. Montaño could send you other recovered animals with the same brand, but they are in such an exhausted condition that they should not travel.

I request that you return all of this property to me in care of the bearer of this letter after jotting down the pertinent evidence and information. I regret that I cannot release to you the "faithful" Negislé until he makes a formal and written declaration to me of the crimes of those of his following.

God and Liberty!
Francisco Narbona

November 25, 1844
Janos, Chihuahua
Military Commandancy of Janos

To the commander of the force from Sonora:

I have reviewed the material evidence you sent me earlier today and am now returning these items in care of your envoys.

Your gratuitous inference that I might in some way be responsible for these thefts does not impress me in the least. I cannot be accountable for the Apaches when they are on such forays. For their part, no law or regulation binds them to report to me before they leave or when they return.

Although you mention nothing about my ultimatum for your departure, I presume that you are leaving today, based on your promise during our face-to-face conversation last evening.

I must continue to insist that Negislé has done no harm to the people of Sonora. Your very admission that the horse in his possession was turned over to my authority by Elías González is proof enough that even if Negislé stole the horse from me—which I would certainly know about—the crime was committed in my department and under my jurisdiction, not yours. Thus I repeat my demand that your peace-abiding prisoner be turned over to me. Least of all do you have any necessity, reason, or right to take Negislé to Sonora to make the declaration you claim you need.[8]

God and Liberty!
Mariano Rodríguez Rey

36

Frustrated Plans and the State of the Apache Frontier

1845

Upon his return to Sonora from Janos, Francisco Narbona reported to his immediate superior, Colonel Elías González, on December 3, 1844. By this time, General Urrea, after a year of demotion by the national government in an attempt to stop the Gándara-Urrea war, was in Hermosillo and once again in full charge of the Sonoran government. All of the details of the Chihuahua situation were forwarded to him, and he immediately rushed a higher-ranking officer, Francisco's father, Colonel Antonio Pascual Narbona, to Fronteras to face the Chihuahua threat.

Meanwhile, Mangas Coloradas, the ranking war chief of the southern Apaches, was wreaking psychological revenge on the pesky Sonorans who were disturbing profitable Apache commerce in Chihuahua. He had a frightening message sent to the incoming Colonel Narbona at Fronteras that he was organizing a gigantic war party in the Chiricahua Mountains to invade Sonora and make captives of entire Sonoran families.

Now that the Papago war was over and the Gándara opposition quieted for the moment, Urrea, temporarily in Hermosillo, was finally able to turn to the principal concern of his forefathers: Apaches. On the first day of 1845 he wrote to his second cousin in Arizpe, José María Elías González, who was Urrea's adjutant for the northern line: "My sole occupation at the moment is to form a sizable force here to go to the aid of the northern frontier." [1]

On January 13 he signed a decree at Altar, the ancestral home of his family. The traditional system of defense stretched from Altar to Fronteras, 140 miles as the crow flies. Urrea proposed to nearly double the defense line by extending it some 130 miles to Sahuaripa in the southeast in order to protect Sonora's eastern flank against the Chihuahua Apaches. Daily patrols operating out of nine temporary encampments beyond the frontier would be manned by civilian militia rotating among the many civilian settlements protected by the line. The list of commanders reads like a militia Who's Who for the northern line. This was certainly the most extensive plan of defense in the history of Sonora.[2]

The "Operational Plan to Cover the Frontier from Altar to Sahuaripa for Defense against Apache Invasion" was signed by Urrea at Ures on February 2, 1845, and published in El Voto de Sonora *on May 8. By then, however, it was much too late to put Urrea's excellent plan into operation. Politics had once again foiled the military genius of Tucson's famous son.*

Urrea's reappointment as governor and departmental military commander in the spring of 1844 was the result of a resolution by Sonora's legislature. It appeared that President José Joaquín Herrera would automatically confirm the legislature's appointment, especially since Urrea had the support of the minister of war, Pedro García Conde, a native of Arizpe. For reasons that are still not entirely clear, Herrera dallied, and it was not until late February 1845 that he sent General Francisco Duque to Sonora to oversee another change in government.

On April 10, 1845, Urrea surrendered all claim to power in Sonora. Providentially, he had just been elected in Durango to a senatorial post in the national assembly, for which he departed some months later, never to return to his native Sonora. This departure was further embittered on September 14 by the death of his wife in Mazatlán (see chapter 38). Subsequently and finally, his brilliant showing as a light-cavalry commander in the Mexican American War spelled the end of his illustrious military career. He died in a cholera epidemic in Durango in 1849. Duque kept Elías González at Arizpe because of his unrivaled knowledge and experience with the northern line. On April 30 the old Arizpeño stubbornly submitted to Duque a plan for a counteroffensive against the Apaches. Although it would suffer the same fate as that of Urrea, what interests us more — because it comprises the document that follows this lengthy commentary — was that he included the best and most complete report of the decade on the military status of the frontier at this critical stage of our desert's history. It is unparalleled in detail and significance.

Arizpe
April 30, 1845

To General Francisco Duque, Military Commander
of the Department of Sonora:

Notes on the Present Status of Sonora's Northern Military Line

A. *Our Frontier Military Companies*
Allow me to begin by giving you the number of men authorized and required
for each frontier company, as contrasted with the numbers they actually have:

1. The authorized and required strength of our presidio at FRON-
   TERAS is 94 men; they have 87.
2. That of our presidio at SANTA CRUZ is also 94; they have 81.
3. The TUCSON presidio, like the two above, requires 94; 78 is all
   they have.
4. The presidio at ALTAR is short by 89 men. They should have
   94; they have only 5.
5. Although the BAVISPE company is authorized 81, they have
   less than half that number, only 32.
6. TUBAC is even worse off, with only 28 of a required 81.
7. Because of the importance of ARIZPE, its active company enjoys the highest quota, 100 men; they have half that number.
8. BACOACHI, like Tubac and Bavispe, is restricted to the lesser
   quota of 81; they have only 53.

Thus for a grand total we are down by well over half: 20 officers and 451 men
out of a required number of 44 officers and 947 men.

There was a time when we were able to station detachments at Babocómari, San Pedro, Los Alisos, Batepito, and Los Hornos in addition to our regular presidio sites. This was so effective that not one Apache was able to get
through to the interior of Sonora at that time.

Now, however, the Apaches are attacking in such great numbers that it
would be very dangerous to keep small detachments away from our towns.
Despite these changed circumstances, we continue periodically to cover such
important points as San Pedro and Batepito.

B. Arms and Ammunition

What weapons we have here on the frontier appear to be in reasonably good condition, but there are enough to go around only because of the reduced number of personnel. Of course, more arms will be needed if we hope to fill vacancies or form new companies.

For this purpose there are arms enough—or almost enough—scattered in the towns. The local authorities and citizens, however, would be reluctant to give them up and should not give them up until the frontier is better protected.

There are some weapons in store at Ures and Hermosillo that could be put to use.

The companies at Fronteras, Santa Cruz, Tucson, and Bavispe are the only ones with artillery pieces, but these are badly mounted. The only useful piece is the four-pounder at Tucson. There is an eight-pounder at Fronteras, but it is troublesome. The auxiliaries at Altar have a smaller piece in good condition. Most of our cavalrymen have lances, and more are presently being manufactured at Arizpe.

Our most important need is to supply each cavalryman with three good horses. The Fronteras, Santa Cruz, and Tucson presidios have 240 cavalrymen but only 200 horses—and even these are unfit for any journey over thirty miles. A central horse herd should be maintained in the lush San Pedro Valley. It could be protected by a good officer and 75 men drawn from all three aforementioned presidios.

Few of our cavalrymen have sufficient training, and even fewer of our officers can impart it. The situation calls for immediate attention. On the other hand, our three infantry companies are in a good state of discipline. I WOULD EVEN PIT THEM AGAINST THE ARMIES OF NAPOLEON.

C. An Added Suggestion

The sizable community of peaceful Apaches, settled at Tucson for decades, should be established as a formal town. It should have its own law and order and be governed by the Apaches themselves. For this purpose it should be further removed from both the presidio and Tucson's Pima Indian village but still be able to play its traditional role in Tucson's defense.

God and Liberty!
José María Elías González

37
National Politics
in Tucson Once Again

1845

The following document once again features Tucson's perennial hero, Antonio Comadurán, still the presidial commander but now civil justice of the peace as well.

Tucson's preference for federalism in 1824 continued throughout the presidial era. The reason was explained in the introduction to chapter 14, including the rationale for its change in April 1834 to centralism and the entrenchment of Antonio López de Santa Anna in power.

Now, some ten years later, for its very survival Tucson radically changed its stand once again and denounced Santa Anna and his brand of centralism. Without proclaiming total local independence, as did Texas and Yucatán, stronger words against Mexico City were never spoken in Mexican Tucson than at this historic meeting on January 20, 1845, in the barracks of the Tucson presidio.

On no other document of the time do we find a more complete and informative list of signatures, representing Tucson's prominent residents, both civilian and military. Note the assembly's unanimous vote for Paredes and the Plan of Guadalajara, and also the unanimous vote for the retention of General José Urrea as governor of Sonora.

January 20, 1845
Tucson, Sonora
Military Commandancy of Tucson

At a meeting on this day in the barracks of the presidio at Tucson, ANTONIO COMADURÁN, first justice of the peace and military commander of our section of the line, spoke in the presence of our retired officers, Loreto Ramírez and Manuel Orozco, and all of the settlers and soldiers of our area.

He characterized the present administration of the Republic of Mexico as hopeless. He also described this as common knowledge. Our leaders pay no attention to even the most basic of their own laws. Weary of taxes and other burdens placed on them for no good reason, our people feel that the nation has lost its sovereignty and independence. To say that we are Mexicans means nothing anymore.

The only remedy for this situation is a plan for positive renewal pronounced at Guadalajara by the most excellent General Mariano Paredes de Arrillaga on the first day of November of last year. His plan reflects not only his own noble and sacred ideals but also the will of the entire nation. As proof of this, the military plaza at Mazatlán and a number of military posts and settlements of our own department have already seconded this plan of Guadalajara.

These various pronouncements were read to the entire assembly. By unanimous vote the following resolutions were passed:

1. The military company of this plaza and its settlers shall adhere to the entire plan—and each of its parts—proposed at Guadalajara on the first of November of last year by the most excellent General Mariano Paredes de Arrillaga.

2. As commander-in-chief of the civil and military government of our department, only our most excellent General José Urrea shall be recognized.

3. The military company of this plaza and its settlers refuse to take the oath to a decree of the central government dated November 29 of last year. We shall swear only to the Organic Bases of the Republic, which, as their most important implication, favor representation at the center from all parts of the nation.[1]

[signatures:]

Captain Antonio Comadurán; Ensign Loreto Ramírez, retired; Ensign Manuel Orozco, retired; Ensign Lorenzo Rodríguez, signing for the auxiliary militia of Altar; Bautista Romero, signing for the grade of sergeant; Solano León, signing for the grade of corporal; Juan Martínez, signing for the soldiers.

Settlers: Ignacio Sáenz, Second Justice of the Peace; Teodoro Ramírez; José Grijalva; Clemente Telles; Luis Burruel; Gerónimo González; Pascual Cruz; Joaquín Comadurán; Miguel Pacheco; Jesús María Ortiz; Ramón Castro; Juan María Santa Cruz; Francisco Granillo; Tomás Ortiz; Juan José Azedo; José Paulino Castro; Ramón Pacheco; Miguel Ignacio Elías; José Grijalva, signing for fifty settlers who do not know how to sign.

> [signature] Solano León, as appointed secretary for the proceedings

38

† The Death of
María Arana de Urrea

The date April 10, 1845, marked the end of General Urrea's power in Sonora. We know that for some months he stayed on in Sonora before leaving for his senatorial post in Durango. The death of his beloved wife, María Arana de Urrea, in Mazatlán on September 14, 1845, came at a very difficult time in the general's life and may have been the occasion of Urrea's final farewell to his native region.

The necrology in El Centinela de Sonora, published in Ures on October 10, 1845, together with an accompanying sonnet, tells us a great deal about the general as well as his wife. We publish it here as an important document in our series, since it one of the few that features feminine involvement in the events of the era.

The eulogy is tantamount to a short biography describing both the general and his wife through the stormy years of his fight for federalism and his two major imprisonments, first in Perote Prison and later in the former headquarters of the Spanish Inquisition in Mexico City.

José and María Urrea had two surviving children. His son, Antonio R. Urrea, of Mazatlán, collaborated in the historical research of Hubert Howe Bancroft during the second half of the last century. He taught at Santa Clara University and has descendants in the Bay area today. Described in the eulogy as "the final fruit of her luckless love," was Antonio R. Urrea this last child of María de Jesús Arana?

Necrology

We regret to announce that María de Jesús Arana de Urrea, wife of Brigadier General José Urrea, died at the port city of Mazatlán on September 14 and is mourned by her grieving husband and family. She was a model of fidelity and devotedness, and was her husband's only joy during the many bitter moments of his heroic career.

Since she could not join him on the battlefield, she could never share in the glory of his successes. It was only in his hours of adversity that she could drink with him from his chalice of bitterness, and she did so to the last drop. She was his consoling angel in the dark recesses of Perote Prison and the dungeons of the Inquisition. It was she who lifted his heavy chains to lighten their burden with her love. She ever pleaded his cause, whether for mercy or for justice, before the inexorable villains of a tyrannical state who for perhaps the first time in their lives could not but be touched by the sincerity of her tears. Whenever she rejoiced at seeing him free, he was once again torn from her loving embrace. After so many cruel separations, the greatest joy of her life finally came in following him into exile, for his appointment to Sonora was so considered at the time. At least here in the remotest corner of the republic she could finally savor the joy of his delightful company, or so she thought.

The envy, ambition, and calumny that greeted him here soon turned her sweet dream into a nightmare, and in the silence of its aftermath a thousand other misfortunes befell her. In terror she witnessed the repeated attempts on her husband's life.

In despair she beheld her children in want and misery, followed by the death-dealing disease that cruelly ended the all too brief lives of two of her three daughters. In a desperate attempt to save the life of the third, she was once again forced to leave the side of her life's companion. We saw with our own eyes her departure by sea at Guaymas, leaving the light of her life alone on the shore. We could almost hear the breaking of her heart and feel the wetness of her tears. We never dreamed, however, that this would be her last farewell. Death awaited her in Mazatlán. Yet, she was able to give birth to the last fruit of her luckless love, before she descended to her eternal tomb.

A valiant general, who never uttered the least cry of complaint amidst whistling bullets in the tempest of war, is now shedding copious tears amidst a myriad of tender and everlasting memories. The editors of *El Centinela*, deeply moved by his loss, wish to share in his sorrow just as we have always stood by him against his malicious enemies.

Thus we dedicate the following sonnet to the virtue, valor, and tenderness of his loving wife, María de Jesús Arana. May her gentle soul rest in peace!

Sonnet

Heartless Parca,[1] tyrant unrelenting,
Spurning even exalted virtue,
So recently has separated from the living
A wife esteemed and ever faithful.

MARÍA JESÚS ARANA, soul of kindness!
Thy mourners' hearts are breaking
With a pain beyond all telling,
For thou art gone, and are no more.

Thy spouse beyond consoling, great URREA,
So bitter and bewildered,
Contemplates thine absence and thy loss.

Recalling now thy love and tenderness,
He lifts his eyes to Heaven
With hope of your reunion there.

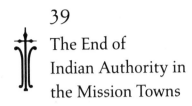

39

The End of
Indian Authority in
the Mission Towns

1846

With appreciation, and even a degree of local pride, we visit the romantic sites of the old Spanish missions in southern Arizona and northern Sonora. Many of the graceful old buildings still possess much of their ancient splendor. But today the original life and daily routine that surrounded them, with all of the living details, escape the eye — those details are gone forever. Exactly when and how did they cease to be? The following two pieces of correspondence, which furnish some answers while raising new questions, partially solve the mystery.

October 18, 1846
Átil in the Altar Valley

To the legal authorities of the prefecture of Altar:

We, native sons of the towns of Oquitoa, Átil, and Tubutama, appear before your tribunal, asserting our full rights and the preference our petitions traditionally enjoy. We justifiably complain at the manner in which mission lands—from time immemorial controlled, cared for, and worked by our forebears, both our spiritual and natural fathers—are now being taken over by private citizens without the concurrence of or consultation with our official missionary. He, in turn, should have full rights over the proceeds from those lands for the repair of our churches, the material needs of divine worship, compensation for the religious instruction of our children, and with even more reason, the

repair and reconstruction of the residential rooms within the mission buildings themselves.

Instead, all these benefits are going to the private citizens usurping the
rights to our own lands. Justice demands that these lands immediately be returned to the administration of our missionary.

To this petition each of us signs his name, accompanied by his rubric.[1]

> Benito Valverde [rubric]
> General Juan Tereso Álamo
> [rubric]
> Governor Cristóbal Aliso [rubric]

October 20, 1846

To the native governors of Oquitoa, Átil, and Tubutama:

On June 14 of this year, a disposition was made by the departmental assembly
of Sonora that all revenue resulting from the use of lands formerly under the
administration of the Indian missions now be transferred to a fund supporting
a school and a teacher for the education of the young people of this political
district, including those coming in from smaller towns.[2] This disposition was
approved by the superior government of this department, which places this
matter beyond the competence of the present judges. The present petitioners
would have to have recourse to His Excellency the Governor himself.[3]

As to the competence of the local diocesan or parish priest in this matter,
the National Decree of March 5, 1845, relieved him of any jurisdiction over the
aforementioned lands and their emoluments. Other expenses of the mission
mentioned by the petitioners would be left to his private zeal and resources,
with no right to profit from former mission lands for the purpose.

In confirmation of which, we, the local justices of the peace for the Altar
political district, affix our rubricked signatures:

> Diego Moreno [rubric]
> José María Bustamante [rubric]

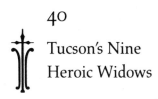

40

Tucson's Nine Heroic Widows

By the beginning of 1848, the Mexican American War was drawing to a close. The conflict's financial effect on the Sonoran frontier, however, was just beginning to be felt. In February, the Sonoran state government had to suspend the bimonthly wheat rations provided to Tucson's presidial soldiers. By early May, Tucson's soldiers and civilians decided upon an emergency strategy to fend off starvation. On May 10, a small expeditionary party of some fifteen settlers and soldiers headed for the abandoned Babocómari rancho, some sixty miles southeast of Tucson, to butcher and bring home to Tucson whatever wild cattle might still be roaming there.

As the Tucsonans rode southward along the western shadow of the Mustang Mountains, an unusually large band of marauding Apaches was waiting in ambush at a water hole only a few miles north of the Babocómari, where the Tucsonans were sure to stop. With an overwhelming advantage of numbers and possessing the element of surprise, the Apaches killed every man of the Tucson expedition.

Nine members of the expedition were military men, married and with families. Our first document is perhaps the most revealing. It contains the petition of the widows for the military pension to which they were entitled. The touching petitions are introduced by a covering letter from Antonio Comadurán, the presidial commander, dated the same day, July 6, 1848, and explaining the terms of the pension.

July 6, 1848
The Tucson Presidio

To Manuel María Gándara at Ures, Commander General of Sonora:

The women who have written the following petition are the widows of the soldiers of the military company who were killed by Apaches in the ambush at the springs at the foot of the Mustang Mountains on May 10 of this year. The purpose of the tragic expedition is also explained in the petition.

They are asking for reinstatement of their regular biweekly allotment of provisions, just as when their husbands were still alive, as well as any extra donation you could add to clothe their families. Naturally, since the death of their husbands they have shouldered alone all responsibility for their families. They would also like to know if they qualify for monetary pensions. In my opinion, sir, I feel that they do qualify both for provisions and a pension. I believe that Your Excellency's opinion will be the same and that you will do all in your power to help these women who have lost their loved ones and now endure hunger, poverty, and total neglect. Your Excellency will arrange what is best for all, I am confident.

Widows' Petition
We, the undersigned widows of Corporal Zeferino Luque, Corporal Juan Rodríguez, Drummer Ignacio Camacho, Soldier Pedro Urías, Soldier Tomás Ocoboa, Soldier Juan Martínez, Soldier Manuel Rodríguez, and Soldier Manuel Castillo are writing to Your Excellency with all respect and submission to your decision:

Since last February [1848], when the biweekly allotment of provisions was discontinued,[1] our families have suffered extreme privation. Finally, our children's hunger forced our husbands to escort a group of Tucson residents to the Babocómari rancho. Our husbands would be paid in foodstuffs promised them by the leader of the settlers.

Enemy Apaches attacked and killed them all last May 10. Since that time, we and our families have suffered hunger and have no money for clothing. God has been our only recourse in our unhappy situation after the death of our husbands.

Now we turn to you in the hope that, with your well-known kindness of heart, you will come to our aid by once again allotting us our provisions every fifteen days and granting us a small donation so that we may clothe ourselves and our families.

As it is now, we are forced to stay indoors to hide our nakedness. It is for this reason that we appeal to your charity that out of love for Our Lord you will receive our petition. We are like orphans who beg God, their father, for assistance. According to royal decree, since their fathers died in battle, their families now deserve a military pension to cover their needs. If this is not the case, we ask you to let us know so that we will not continue to hope for such help.[2]

Tucson, July 6, 1848

Signatures:

Luisa Huerta, widow of Corporal Luque

Tomasa Toysoque, widow of Corporal Rodríguez

Magdalena Butierras, widow of Drummer Ignacio Camacho

Ramona González, widow of Pedro Urías

Antonia Siqueiros, widow of Tomás Ocoboa

Mariana Romero, widow of Juan Martínez

Petra Ocoboa, widow of Rafael Ramírez

María Telles, widow of Manuel Rodríguez

Francisca Bayesteros, widow of Manuel Castillo

Notes

Foreword

1. See *A Spanish Frontier in the Enlightened Age*, Publications of the Academy of American Franciscan History, Monograph Series, vol. 13 (Washington, D.C.: Academy of American Franciscan History, 1981).

Introduction

The following sources were employed in writing the Introduction: Francisco R. Almada, *Diccionario de historia, geografía y biografía sonorenses* (Hermosillo: Gobierno del Estado de Sonora, 1983); Laureano Calvo Berber, *Nociones de historia de Sonora* (Mexico City: Librería de Manuel Porrúa, 1958); James E. Officer, *Hispanic Arizona, 1536–1856* (Tucson: University of Arizona Press, 1987); Vicente Riva Palacio, *Resumen integral de México a través de los siglos*, vol. 4: *México independiente, 1821–1855*, abridged by Enrique Olavarria y Ferrari (Mexico City: Compañía General de Ediciones, 1974); Juan Domingo Vidargas del Moral, *Historia general de Sonora*, vol. 2: *De la conquista al estado libre y soberano de Sonora*, chap. 11: "Sonora y Sinaloa como provincias independientes y como Estado Interno de Occidente" (Hermosillo: Gobierno del Estado de Sonora, 1985).

Chapter 1. Tucson's First Civilian Mayor Reports

The original document is in the Archivo Histórico del Estado de Sonora, Hermosillo, Mexico, Asuntos Indígenas: Apaches.

1. The section of Spanish and later Mexican Tucson known as El Pueblito was the Pima village at the foot of Sentinel Peak on the west bank of the Santa Cruz River. This was the original native village and mission of Tucson, which became a satellite of the village and mission of San Xavier del Bac many years before the presidio and Spanish settlement invaded the east bank of the river.

2. The Apache military company under Chief Antuna was without a doubt the most important adjunct of the Tucson military force. For the settlement of peaceful Apaches at Tucson, see *Desert Documentary*, 61–64, 134–135.

Chapter 2. New Information about Captain José Romero

1. Los Angeles: Ward and Ritchie Press.

2. James E. Officer, *Hispanic Arizona, 1536–1856* (Tucson: University of Arizona Press, 1987), 90.

Chapter 3. The Eyes and Ears of Occidente on the Gila

This translation was made from a typescript in the Bancroft Library, Berkeley, California, M-A 19, pt. 1, 0002. The Bancroft typescript, in turn, bears a note saying that it was transcribed from the original in the Archivo Histórico del Estado de Sonora, on January 11, 1911 (by Bolton?). A recent search failed to locate the original.

Chapter 4. The First Americans in Tucson

Translated from the original, signed and rubricated by Juan Romero; Archivo Histórico del Estado de Sonora, Asuntos Indígenas: Apaches.

Chapter 5. The Old Pueblo in Peril

Translated from the original, signed and rubricated by Juan Romero; Archivo Histórico del Estado de Sonora, Asuntos Indígenas: Apaches.

Chapter 6. Manuel Escalante Defends Tucson

Translated from the original manuscript, signed and rubricated by Manuel Escalante y Arvizu; Archivo Histórico del Estado de Sonora, Asuntos Indígenas.

Chapter 7. Armageddon in the Missions

My discovery of this document was a find indeed. It was my good fortune to be a member of the official Mexican team searching for the grave of Father Eusebio Kino in 1966. In response to our request locally for old Spanish documents in private hands that might aid us in our search, the well-known Campbell family of Magdalena allowed me to copy this family heirloom, an early copy of the signed original. It is the sole extant key to the total reality behind the tragedy of 1828. It is still considered secret enough that it is retained in private hands.

Chapter 8. Manuel Escalante Defends the Missions

Translated from the original manuscript, signed and rubricated by Manuel Escalante y Arvizu; Archivo Histórico del Estado de Sonora, Asuntos Indígenas.

Chapter 9. The Return of the Missions to the Franciscans

Edited and translated from the original manuscript; Archivo Histórico del Estado de Sonora, cabinet 1, drawer 1, folder 149.

Chapter 10. A Pima Prophecy

This document was originally published in *The Americas,* 34 (October 1977): 159. The original manuscript, written, signed, and rubricated by the Indian author, is in the Archivo Histórico del Estado de Sonora, Asuntos Indígenas: Pápagos.

Chapter 11. Changes in the Structure of Town Government

Edited and translated from Pinart Print 243, an original printed circular in the Bancroft Library.

Chapter 12. Apacheland Explodes

Translated from the original manuscript in the Archivo Histórico del Estado de Sonora, Asuntos Indígenas.

1. During the night a few weeks later, some fifty Pinal warriors, mostly relatives and followers of Nagayé, the deceased Pinal war captain, suddenly appeared outside the presidio gate and raced around the walls without attacking. Since the Apaches did not fight at night, the demonstration symbolized that the score had been evened. Perhaps it was Nagayé himself who had killed the Tucson warrior during the parley.

Chapter 13. The Patriotic Section

The Chihuahua state circular, translated here, is in the Archivo Histórico del Estado de Sonora, cabinet 2, drawer 3.

Chapter 14. Mexican National Politics in Tucson

Translated from an early manuscript copy; Bancroft Library, Documents relating to Northern Mexico, series 2, item 60.

Chapter 15. An Apache Woman Reports

Translated from an early copy, dated July 6, 1834; Archivo Histórico del Estado de Sonora, Asuntos Indígenas: Apaches.

1. Our document corrects a current belief that Sabino Canyon, a popular recreation area northeast of Tucson, is named after Sabino Otero, an early rancher in that area. Since our manuscript precedes Sabino Otero's birth by more than a decade, the plentiful juniper (*sabino*) trees there must have given occasion for its present name long before.

2. The copper mines of Santa Rita del Cobre in southwestern New Mexico near present day Silver City were the scene of the exchange of arms and ammunition for stolen mules. They were within forty miles of the rebel stronghold in the Mogollón Mountains. In 1836 the Sonoran government entertained legal action against Robert McKnight, an American and co-owner of the mines, for arming hostile Apaches.

Chapter 16. Tubac Undefended

Translated from the original manuscript in the Archivo Histórico del Estado de Sonora, Asuntos Indígenas: Apaches.

1. For a parallel description in Spanish times, see *Desert Documentary: The Spanish Years, 1767–1821*, pp. 31–34.

Chapter 17. Escalante's Massive Offensive Begins

Translated from the original manuscript in the Archivo Histórico de Sonora, Asuntos Indígenas: Apaches.

1. La Playa de los Pimas, now known as Willcox Playa, is a large, dry lakebed fifty miles northeast of the Babocómari.

2. Escalante concluded that, with their simplistic tradition of offering the enemy a treaty before they were attacked, New Mexico and Chihuahua would have ruined the whole campaign. The elements at Santa Rita del Cobre who were arming the renegades in exchange for mules would certainly have directed the regional political authorities to arrange for a treaty, which the renegades would hurriedly

accept but then disregard. The Sonorans, who were of another jurisdiction, would have nothing to say about it.

Escalante was quite intentionally manipulating Article 4 of his authorization from the Sonoran legislature requiring him to coordinate the campaign with New Mexico and Chihuahua. He cleverly feigned compliance by instructing his vice-governor to inform New Mexico and Chihuahua only after it would be too late to stop his final approach to the Mogollóns.

3. Escalante's boldness is quite apparent. He would move all of his supplies and remounts into the San Simón Valley, a hundred miles from their base camp on the Babocómari but only sixty miles from the Mogollón Mountains. There was no turning back.

Chapter 18. Victory in the Mogollóns

Translated from the original manuscript in the Archivo Histórico del Estado de Sonora, Asuntos Indígenas: Apaches.

1. Tutijé was one of the original ringleaders of the rebellion of peaceful Apaches in 1832, which began at the Chihuahua presidio of Janos.

2. Throughout the great campaign, these "brave men" were civilian volunteers or members of local or active militias. This was a state, not a federal, project. Escalante had no authority to command regular presidio soldiers, who were so few in number that they were all needed to protect the presidial settlements.

3. Documents in later chapters reveal that two other Janero war captains were captured by Sonoran forces. The three captives should have been turned over to authorities in Chihuahua, who had jurisdiction over Janos and the Janos Apaches. In such an event, however, the three would doubtlessly have been pardoned by one of the perennial Chihuahua "peace treaties" and would have lived to take vengeance on Sonora. Thus, Tutijé was executed at Arizpe almost immediately. The other two suffered the same fate, one at Fronteras and the other at Santa Cruz. To avenge the death of their leaders, the Janos Apaches set up a regular raiding pattern from across the Chihuahua border into Sonora that lasted well into the 1840s.

Chapter 19. The Papagos Turn to Raiding

Translated from the original manuscript in the Archivo Histórico del Estado de Sonora, Asuntos Indígenas: Papagos, cuaderno 6.

1. The Quijotoa Mountains are centrally located on the Tohono O'odham reservation today. The village referred to in the narrative, whose governor intervened for the Mexican troops, was probably *ma'ishch wawhia* (Covered Wells), a promi-

nent village at the northern end of the Quijotoas and today a crossroads for the reservation.

Chapter 20. Tucson Makes Peace with the Pinal Apaches

Translated from an early copy in the Archives of the Franciscan headquarters of the Michoacán Franciscan Province, Celaya, Guanajuato, Mexico.

1. Sonora is referred to as a department rather than a state because of the October 1835 decree by the national congress converting the Republic to a centralist form of government. Escalante continued as provisional governor, but the department was ruled by a five-man junta. The previous "state congress" was dissolved.

Chapter 21. The Aftermath of the Pinal Peace Treaty

Translated from the original manuscript in the Archivo Histórico del Estado de Sonora, Asuntos Indígenas: Apaches.

Chapter 22. Tucson's Storekeeper Diplomat

Translated from the original Ramírez manuscript and a draft copy of the covering letter in the Archivo Histórico del Estado de Sonora, Asuntos Indígenas: Papagos, cuaderno 9.

1. The promise to Azul had obviously been made prior to the Pinal peace treaty of March 5, 1836 (q.v.). The practice of tribes allied with the Spaniards presenting enemy ears as symbols of loyalty and as deserving of reward went back to the early years of the Conquest. In defense of commander Martínez, he himself had signed the Pinal peace treaty and could hardly be expected personally to aid the Gila Pimas in their frequent and traditional attacks on their neighbors, the Pinal Apaches.

Chapter 23. An American Fortress on the Upper Gila

Translated from an early handwritten copy in the Archivo Histórico del Estado de Sonora, cabinet 7, drawer 1, folder 86.

1. By the time Arizpe was buzzing with the formidable rumor in September 1837, the Americans—fortress and all—had been gone for nearly a year.

Chapter 24. Greedy Goldseekers and Papago Gold

Translated from the original manuscripts in the Archivo Histórico del Estado de Sonora, cabinet 7, drawer 2, folder 92.

1. Quitovac is a Papago village some thirty miles south of Sonoyta, Sonora, and

Lukeville, Arizona, the point of entry between the United States and Mexico on the international border. Neighboring Quitovac to the west was the site of San Antonio, where gold was first discovered in the Papago country in 1834. Quitovac also had—and still has—the mining advantage of a small lake to the west between Quitovac and San Antonio.

2. The Piman word *tonlig* (pronounced tó-no-lic) has the applied meaning here of "giver of light," an appropriate nickname for a wise leader.

3. San Perfecto, about forty miles northwest of Altar, was a Mexican mining camp and seat of Mexican authority in that part of the Papago country in the Sonoran political district of Altar. The author of this letter, Santiago Redondo, was the prefect of the Altar political district, and his representative at San Perfecto—known as a "justice"—was Ramón Oviedo, whom we shall meet later in this chapter.

4. Redondo, a civil servant, had no jurisdiction over the military presidio at Altar. His "auxiliary company" therefore was composed of civilian settlers.

5. *Cubó* was the Spanish rendering of the name of the present Papago village and district of Gu Vo in the southwest corner of the present U.S. Tohono O'odham Reservation.

6. Soñi was an important mining camp as late as 1848 and after. Today the nearby and better-known Mexican mining settlement of El Plomo still has more than 600 residents. Many of the longtime residents of Mexican Tubac settled at Soñi after Tubac was abandoned under Apache pressure in 1848. Today, Soñi is the site of a Mexican rancho about seventy miles south of the present international border.

7. Carricito was only a few miles southeast of the mining town of San Perfecto. There were mines in the area of both towns. The justice at San Perfecto wanted to use the Carricito water for all of these mines. Diego Celaya, however, was the prime offender in grazing his livestock on the land of the Carricito Papagos.

Chapter 25. The Battle of Cóbota

Translated from a contemporary copy in the Archivo Histórico del Estado de Sonora, Asuntos Indígenas: Papagos, cuaderno 15.

1. The Centralist government of 1837 divided Sonora into nine political districts, or prefectures, headed by prefects, to which the settlements of the district answered. The prefects acted as liaisons with the supreme state government.

Chapter 26. Papago Unrest Reaches Tucson

Translated from the original Comadurán letter in the Bancroft Library, Documents relating to Northern Mexico, series 3, item 38.

1. La Sierra de la Madera was the traditional Hispanic name for the Santa Rita Mountains, the prominent range visible to the southeast of Tucson. Its English translation as "timber mountains" assures us that it was the source of much of the wood used in early construction in both Tucson and Tubac.

2. This was high tribute to the military discipline of the presidio's strongest adjunct, the peaceful Apaches. They refused to fight because they had received no order to fight.

Chapter 27. Quitovac under Siege

Translated from the original in the Archivo Histórico del Estado de Sonora, cabinet 8, drawer 1.

1. Martínez is referring to the nefarious activity of Manuel María Gándara, who near the start of 1842 had been forced out of the governorship by the clever political maneuvering of General Urrea. The action of Urrea, a Federalist, was legal and had the surprising concurrence of Centralist president Antonio López de Santa Anna. In retaliation, Gándara secretly stirred up rebellion among both the Yaquis and the Papagos solely to spite his perennial enemy, Urrea.

Chapter 28. Tucson Girds for Defense

The three original letters are at the Bancroft Library, Documents relating to Northern Mexico, series 3, items 47, 48, 49.

1. Urrea, Comadurán, and José María Elías González were close relatives. Their blood ties stemmed from the Elías González and Díaz del Carpio families, which had pioneered the far northern frontier during the previous century. With Arizpe as their base, their commitment was to presidios and the far northern line. In opposition, the Gándaras centered around Ures and favored the business interests of central Sonora. These family relationships are the key to understanding most of Sonora's political squabbles during this period.

2. The correct name and identity of this emissary will be revealed in the third letter in this series. See note 6, below.

3. An English equivalent for this name would be Yaqui John or Yaqui Jack, since *Yoreme* is the name the Yaquis have traditionally used for themselves.

4. The Tubac log for February 21, 1843, records that early that morning three raiding Apaches stole a horse herd from Sópori, the mining and agricultural settlement between Tubac and Arivaca. The settlers there gave chase and also sent word ahead to San Xavier del Bac. The San Xavier people caught up with the Apaches at

a place called El Amole, recovered the horse herd, and killed one of the Apaches—whose scalp enjoyed the place of honor in the scalp dance at San Xavier referred to in our letter (Roque de Ibarra, commander at Tubac, "Diario de las novedades ocurridas en el mes anterior," Tubac, March 1, 1843. Bancroft Library, Documents relating to Northern Mexico, series 3, item 45).

5. This sentence solves a mystery of long standing for me. When I completed my term as pastor of the Altar Valley in Mexico in 1965, the people of Oquitoa rewarded me with an eighteenth-century statue of St. Francis of Assisi, which now stands in the museum at San Xavier Mission. I asked why the hands were missing and how it had happened that evidently at one time the head had been severed from the body and then glued back on. I was told that long ago the Papagos had attacked Oquitoa and had sacked the church. As a missionary for twenty-eight years among the peaceful Tohono O'odham (exemplary Christians today with signs of a long tradition as such), I concluded—fortunately without expressing my conviction—that the real culprits must have been the Apaches. I stand corrected.

6. Identified by Culo Azul of the Gila Pimas and Antonio of the Maricopas as a personal representative of Manuel Gándara, "the Indian from Horcasitas named Sósthenes" was in all probability the Sóstomo, or Crisóstomo, mentioned here. Although he may have been contacted in Horcasitas by Gándara to serve as his emissary to the Gila River, his native tongue would preferably have been Piman, to communicate with the Gila Pimas. The Papago suspect in our third letter describes him as a "Christian Papago from Sauz." Abandoned today, Sauz was a Papago village at the foot of the Sauceda Mountains in the northern part of the Hickiwan district of the modern Tohono O'odham reservation.

General Urrea in a letter of September 13, 1843, names Sóstomo as the principal ringleader of the last phase of the Papago War. Urrea cites his place of origin as Bísanig in the Caborca mission district. This would explain his being baptized with San Juan Crisóstomo as his Christian patron saint. Mexican squatters later forced him to migrate to Sauz in the northern Papaguería. All of this undeniably made Sóstomo a prime suspect as a leader in the rebellion, and there was even a rumor that he had made an alliance with Gándara.

Chapter 29. General Urrea's Offensive against the Papagos

Translated from the printed copy in the official state government newspaper, *El Voto de Sonora*, supplement of June 1, 1843. The original manuscript has not been found.

1. Coyote Well is located on Coyote Mountain, which is on the northeast corner

of the Baboquívari Range. There is still an active groundwater spring a few yards up its western slope. The village below is also known as Coyote Village, or Bandak (Place of the Coyote).

2. The Artesa village and mountains are some fifteen miles west northwest of Fresnal Canyon.

3. Antonio Urrea reappears later as prefect of the Altar political district in 1850 and 1851.

4. The Cababi, or Ko Vaya, Mountains are some twelve miles north northwest of Artesa.

5. We have found no other record to date of Charles Grimes, American or British, in Sonora at this time.

6. As the filibustering expedition of Henry Crabb approached Caborca on the morning of April 1, 1857, Lorenzo Rodríguez, by then a captain, was killed by them when he approached to parley.

Chapter 30. The Immediate Effect of the April Campaign

Translated from the only extant copy of this letter, a printed version in Sonora's official newspaper, *El Voto de Sonora,* Ures, supplement of June 1, 1843.

1. Kohatk is still one of the northernmost Papago villages, with close ties socially and linguistically with the people of the Gila River.

Chapter 31. The Authority of the Papago Governors Is Renewed

1. Antonio Comadurán to José María Elías González, Tucson, October 17, 1844, in the Bancroft Library, Documents relating to Northern Mexico, series 3, item 70.

2. In all probability, Elías González personally commissioned Pedro for this task during the Tucson peace talks.

3. Pirigua, a name no longer used, was the Spanish designation for the Papago village of Hickiwan. The villages of Santa Rosa, Kaka, and Hickiwan still exist today in the northwest portion of the modern Tohono O'odham reservation.

4. A vestige of this custom is still observed in my own mission village of San Xavier del Bac, southwest of Tucson. The celebration of the principal religious feasts of the liturgical year is organized by the feast committee, consisting of twelve men and twelve women. Five distinct feast committees serve by rotation, each for a full year between successive patronal feasts of San Francisco Xavier. The changing of the guard takes place each year on December 4, the day after the patronal feast. In a solemn ceremony, the head of the outgoing committee passes on to the

head of the incoming group a silver-headed black wand or cane of office, which is about two feet long.

5. The Urrea passport is translated from the draft copy in the Archivo Histórico del Estado de Sonora, Asuntos Indígenas: Papagos, cuaderno 29.

Chapter 32. The San Xavier and Tucson Missions

Translated from an official transmission of the original report, on four folios in the Archivo Histórico del Estado de Sonora, cabinet 8, drawer 1, folder 121.

1. The reader may be surprised at reference to the "exiled Jesuits," who had had no contact with these "lands and possessions" for more than three-quarters of a century. Actually, the reference is no more surprising than the very strange decree of Mexico's president, Antonio López de Santa Anna, dated June 21, 1843, entrusting—after three centuries—Mexico's entire northern frontier to the Society of Jesus, now reinstated by the Church, to start the missionization process all over again. The untimely decree was published in *El Voto de Sonora,* which occasioned the state government of Sonora to request the present report.

2. Oral tradition places this "recreational garden" not where the present cloister garden is today—as might be suspected—but extending well behind the apse of the church.

3. For the first time the report introduces the man who might be called the villain of the story. Fray Rafael Díaz, born near Cádiz in 1784, was the unscrupulous individual who unfortunately avoided the Spanish Expulsion of 1828. Our document gives the story in full, referring to him as "the late Fray Rafael," since he had died at San Ignacio two years before the writing of the present report.

4. The image is also known as the Black Christ, since the corpus on the cross is black. It is the object of a popular "private" devotion that had its origin in Guatemala during the Spanish period in connection with miraculous cures. The Tucson image was taken to Imuris, Sonora, during the national changeover, by the retreating troops of the Tucson presidio in 1856. It can still be seen hanging in the church at Imuris.

5. The full name of the Querétaro missionary college, which took over the Pimería Alta missions after the expulsion of the Jesuits in 1767, was the College of the Holy Cross of Querétaro of the Propagation of the Faith (in Latin, Propaganda Fide), which indicates its missionary purpose.

6. Our anonymous reporter, as he himself indicates in his following sentences, was referring to the golden age before all peninsular-born Spaniards, including those who were missionary friars, were expelled from Mexico in 1828 by the Mexi-

can congress, now independent of the Spanish Crown. If someone had pleaded their legal cause, frontier missionaries under the law could have been exempted from expulsion for the sake of Indian peace on the frontier, always a delicate issue. Before 1828, there was generally a Queretaran missionary in every major mission— a factor in judging the circuit-riding friars, who were also Queretarans, after 1828. They were understandably unable to do all of the things expected by the author of this document—and "the late Fray Rafael," was a singular exception even among the circuit-riding Queretarans in his mismanagement of mission property.

7. Our reporter, with his limited vantage point of 1843, perhaps overstates his case when he concludes that the natives who had left the missions and returned to the open desert due to the lack of management, or even because of mismanagement had "abandoned religious practice." When the mission system was in full bloom, and even today, the distant desert villages had and have their tiny chapels for devotion to the saints. As early as 1811, Father Juan Bautista Llorens, builder of the church at San Xavier, noted these chapels during an official visitation of the entire Papago country, as well as the admirable condition the people kept them in. For more information on this devotion away from the formal river missions, see the report of Juan Bautista Llorens to Francisco Moyano, San Agustín del Tucson, December 27, 1811; Querétaro College Archives, Celaya, Guanajuato.

Chapter 33. A Final Report on the Pimería Alta

Translated from a draft copy of the original report at the Bancroft Library, Documents relating to Northern Mexico, series 3, item 62.

1. Roque Ibarra, "Noticias del mes pasado," Tubac, March 1, 1843; Bancroft Library, Documents relating to Northern Mexico, series 3, item 45.

2. Antonio González was born near Morelia, Mexico, on January 1, 1800. He entered the Queretaran college in 1825. His American birth qualified him to replace the Spanish-born friars, exiled in 1828. Coming to the Pimería Alta in 1833, his first assignment was San Xavier del Bac. González's last recorded functions in October of 1843 marked the end of the long Queretaran era in the Pimería Alta, 1768–1843, exactly seventy-five years.

The Franciscans would not officially return to the Pimería Alta for nearly another seventy-five years. Father Bonaventure Oblasser, a Franciscan representing what soon would become the western Franciscan province of the United States of America, took up residence at Mission San Xavier del Bac in 1910. His assignment was to extend the Spanish and Mexican foundations of an earlier Pimería Alta by founding new missions in the waterless Papago country, which had been impossible prior to the invention of modern well-drilling technology. Thus continues the saga of ongoing, and even new, Indian missions in the Pimería Alta. Some Papago families retain an oral tradition of which river towns they ruled under Spain and Mexico.

3. Bartolo Pérez Serrano, prefect of the San Ignacio political district, Cucurpe, July 18, 1844, to the bishop of Sonora and Sinaloa, Lázaro de la Garza y Ballesteros; Archivo Histórico del Estado de Sonora, cabinet 8, drawer 5, folder 146.

4. According to the parish archives of Altar, Sonora, Vázquez was still ministering in the Altar district in 1853. He was a native of the region and had served his parish for fifty-three years, a record by any ecclesiastical standards.

5. Cieneguilla had been an established gold mining town since the early 1770s. A short distance south of Altar, it was Vázquez's home town, and he was evidently residing there when he wrote the report.

6. Later Vázquez assures the bishop that he visited all of the missions and "recovered their living quarters." Yet he fails to mention the Santa Cruz River in his introduction and confuses the church at Tumacácori with the magnificent church at San Xavier.

7. All of these churches of the Pimería Alta, including San Ignacio, Cocóspera, and San Xavier del Bac, were built during the Franciscan period (1768–1843), and have become the trademark of that period in the history of the Pimería Alta.

8. Once again Vázquez was confused. A cursory review of our documentary between July 28, 1828, and May 25, 1830, will readily reveal that beginning with the latter date and ending with the last function of Fray Antonio González in 1843, the friars once again administered the material effects of the missions, including the living quarters.

9. Vázquez related personally to Alday because he was a fellow diocesan priest and, like Vázquez, had been born in Sonora and ordained for the Sonora diocese. He had served as chaplain of the Santa Cruz presidio for less than two years. In early October 1843, the presidial commander, Lt. Manuel Viva, and he were killed in a massive Apache attack on the fort. Alday's untimely death—less than two years into the ministry—was fresh in Vázquez's mind.

10. This valuable report is our only source of information about the existence of libraries in the Pimería Alta. The presence of more than 300 volumes, and perhaps more in other missions, is impressive for this far frontier. Most were probably theological textbooks and pastoral handbooks.

One of the former, from a broken set of moral theology treatises, was still held in the Altar parish office when I was pastor there some thirty years ago. It was originally on loan from the Querétaro missionary college library, as most of the mission volumes probably were. Although not visible as the book stood upright on the shelf, the Querétaro insignia had been branded with a hot iron onto the underside of the volume, cleverly indicating its origin and ownership.

Chapter 34. Could You Have Ridden with Comadurán?

Translated from the two original reports; Bancroft Library, Documents relating to Northern Mexico, series 3, items 64 and 66.

1. Peña Blanca is the white thumb-rock that today overlooks Drexel Heights, a southwest section of modern Tucson. In earlier days, this rock served as an excellent spy-post for enemy Apaches, affording both protection and a clear view of the Tucson area and San Xavier.

2. The Sierrita del Oro is a prominent range running southeast–northwest about forty miles southwest of Tucson. It is known on U.S. maps as the Sierrita Range. An arroyo on its southwest flank still bears the name, used here by Comadurán, of El Champurrado.

3. Since the days of the Spanish reconquest of the Iberian Peninsula from the Muslims, "Santiago!" has been the Spanish battle cry in an attack. The full phrase was "Santiago y a ellos!" or "After them in the name of St. James!" Based on a tradition that St. James the Greater, one of the Twelve Apostles, visited the Compostela area of northern Spain, the kingdoms of the Iberian Peninsula officially chose him as their patron saint. That this ancient Hispanic custom was still observed in the days of Comadurán, a thousand years later, is intriguing.

4. The "natural fortress" is a pass now known as Hell's Gate. It divides the Atascosa Mountains from the Tumacácori range. This protective jumble of huge boulders can easily be reached today by turning west off Interstate 19 at the Peck Canyon turnoff a few miles south of Tumacácori. In the last century, Al Peck had his ranch up that canyon, at the head of which is Hell's Gate.

5. This Babocómari is not to be confused with the other Babocómari along the San Pedro River in southeastern Arizona. This Babocómari is along the Altar River south of Saric.

6. Bearing the same name today, Saucito Mountain protrudes eastward out of the north–south Baboquívari range, commanding an incomparable view of the Altar Valley to the south, whence Comadurán expected the Apaches to come, since they had been raiding in that area.

7. The timing of the attack on Búsanig might indicate that the Pinal war chief accompanied Comadurán back to Tucson as a ruse to allow his war party to allow themselves to be seen heading north toward home by Comadurán's troops and

then to double back to the south to continue their raiding mission in the Altar Valley unmolested. By the time their war chief was on his way home "to influence his people to come to Tucson to settle in peace," his warriors were raiding Búsanig.

8. Finally seeing through the war chief's plot, Comadurán waited patiently on Saucito Mountain, counting on the damage he had already done to the war party. Another possibility, of course, was that the war party would detect Comadurán in the area and come up the west side of the Baboquívari range. That this was in fact what happened was confirmed by the report that awaited Comadurán upon his return to Tucson on September 16. Tracks of the war party and their stolen horse herd had already been observed on the approaches to the Gila River.

9. This second raid on the Búsanig rancho suggests that the first war chief had lied about Quilcedé's destination being Horcasitas and that the latter had planned from the beginning to raid the Búsanig rancho in conjunction with or soon after the first raid, stealing the horses on the first raid and the cattle on the second. For now, the Apaches had completely outwitted the presidials.

10. The Tortuguitas are now known as the Silver Bell Mountains. Tortuga Butte at its southern end is the only vestige of its Hispanic name. The latter was more picturesque, since its chain of gently curving peaks curiously resembles a row of little turtles.

11. Although its full Hispanic name was El Picacho del Gila, it is now known as Picacho Peak (*picacho* means "peak" in Spanish). No regional topographic feature is better known. Unlike other peaks, which are usually attached to complete mountain ranges, it stands alone alongside Interstate 10, the well-traveled highway to Phoenix, some thirty miles north of Tucson.

Chapter 35. Chihuahua Apaches Raid Sonora
Translated from the original and copies of the Narbona–Rey correspondence, in an *expediente*; Bancroft Library, Documents relating to Northern Mexico, series 3, items 72 and 79.

1. Report of Lt. Francisco Durazo to Col. José María Elías González, Guásabas, Sonora, October 12, 1844; Bancroft Library, Documents relating to Northern Mexico, series 3, item 67.

2. Report of Captain Francisco Campillo to Col. José María Elías González, Horcasitas, Sonora, October, 1844; Bancroft Library, Documents relating to Northern Mexico, series 3, item 68.

3. It was common for acting commanders of one presidio to retain the legal commandancy of another.

4. This was the pattern of the Janero operation, as we shall see from later evidence. Within the protection of the Sierra del Enmedio, so-called because it marked the boundary between Sonora and Chihuahua, the raiding party divided the spoils and dispersed to lose their identity as a war party under the friendly skies of Chihuahua. The Sierra del Enmedio, its northern end touching the present international border, is better known today as the San Luis Mountains.

Testimony of Col. Antonio Pascual Narbona, Fronteras, Sonora, December 3, 1844; Bancroft Library, Documents relating to Northern Mexico, series 3, item 73.

5. "Don Roberto" was, of course, the well-known Robert McKnight of the Santa Rita mines in New Mexico, which at this time was mining near Corralitos, Chihuahua. The testimony cited above explains that on the day before the arrival of the Sonorans, McKnight paid the Apaches for the cattle. Out of this consideration, the Sonorans agreed to accept his promise to make payment a second time to the rightful owners.

6. Negislé was from the Mogollón Apache band and came to Janos early on as peace envoy of the Mogollón native "general" Pisago Cabezón in 1840. Whatever involvement he enjoyed with later Janero raiders, which as a respected member of Apache society it was impossible for him to avoid, the Janos commander's arguments in his favor are impressive.

7. Since the source of our Spanish text was copied in an *expediente*, the brand symbols were not reproduced.

8. Narbona, too, was impressed by these arguments and released Negislé before returning to Sonora; see note 6, above.

Chapter 36. Frustrated Plans and the State of the Apache Frontier
Translated from a draft of the original; Bancroft Library, Documents relating to Northern Mexico, series 3, item 81.

1. Among the well-known citizens serving the Sonoran militia as commanders were José María Martínez of Tubac and Ignacio Pesqueira of Arizpe. At the time, Pesqueira was a captain in the militia (at age twenty-four), but in a very few years he would become one of the most powerful political and military figures in the history of Sonora.

2. Urrea to Elías González, Hermosillo, January 1, 1845; Bancroft Library, Documents relating to Northern Mexico, series 3, item 80.

Chapter 37. National Politics in Tucson Once Again
Translated from the original record in the Archivo Histórico del Estado de Sonora, cabinet 8, drawer 5, folder 150.

1. The decree of November 29, 1844, was the final attempt by the besieged government of Santa Anna to save itself. It called for the recognition of Santa Anna as constitutional president of Mexico, the suspension of sessions of the national congress, and the transfer of all powers to the executive branch.

Despite their opportunistic and momentary backing of Paredes' perennial ambition, Tucsonans were basically and prudently only demanding the observance of the Organic Bases of June 12, 1843, which had weakened the Centralist Constitution of 1836 in favor of adequate representation of the provinces in national decisions affecting interests outside of Mexico City.

Chapter 38. Death of María Arana de Urrea

1. Parca, a Roman goddess of death, is still recalled in death announcements throughout the Latin world.

Chapter 39. The End of Indian Authority in the Mission Towns

Translated from the original documents in the Archivo Histórico del Estado de Sonora, cabinet 9, drawer 4, folder 183.

1. This meeting at Átil in the Altar Valley in October 1846 is our only proof that as late as 1846 in the Altar River towns of Oquitoa, Átil, and Tubutama native governors continued to operate within those local Indian communities. We do not know what influence they had over the non-Indians, whose numbers were increasing in these towns at this time.

It is significant that the meeting was held at Átil. Note that the native governor there was General Juan Tereso, who was at that time the state's appointee as commanding general of the entire Papago nation, a role invented by the Sonoran legislature in the 1830s in an attempt to control Papago unrest. Tereso even received the gesture of a monetary reward periodically from the legislature. Even though the arrangement was totally alien to Papago tradition, it seems to have caught the fancy of the natives of Caborca, who still recognize, symbolically, a successor in that role.

2. The three native settlements represented—Oquitoa, Átil, and Tubutama— were, and still are, close to the headquarters of the Altar district.

3. There is no record that the Sonoran governor was ever approached in the matter. By 1846 it had been settled in higher circles of government.

Chapter 40. Tucson's Nine Heroic Widows

Translated from the original documents in the Archivo Histórico del Estado de Sonora, Asuntos Indígenas: Apaches.

1. As explained in the introduction to this document, the deprivation of regular rations to these families began four months before the massacre and was one of many delayed effects of the Mexican American War. The families' plight was of course accentuated by the death of the family breadwinner, who usually followed an agricultural and stock-raising career alongside his military one.

2. In the Hermosillo archives there is a draft copy in the hand of Gándara recommending the petition to the "montepio," or government agency for pensions, as well as an approval of the twenty-five extra pesos as an addition.

Index

About the Editor

Kieran McCarty has a Ph.D. in Latin American history from the Catholic University of America in Washington, D.C. From 1960 through 1965 he worked with the Republic of Mexico under the aegis of the Organization of American States to microfilm documentary sources, with an emphasis on northwestern Mexico and the American Southwest. He was a member of the official team from Mexico City that discovered the grave of folk hero and Jesuit missionary Eusebio Francisco Kino at Magdalena, Sonora, in 1966. In 1976 his book *Desert Documentary: The Spanish Years, 1767–1821* was published by the Arizona Historical Society. *Frontier Documentary* is a sequel to that volume, covering the period from Mexican Independence to the Mexican American War. Well known as a research historian at the University of Arizona since 1980, he is presently historian and archivist for the university's Mexican American Studies & Research Center. His other publications include *A Spanish Frontier in the Enlightened Age*, published by the Academy of American Franciscan History in 1981.